The

Philosopher's

Table

The Philosopher's Table

How to Start Your Philosophy Dinner Club—
Monthly Conversation, Music,
and Recipes

Marietta McCarty

JEREMY P. TARCHER/PENGUIN · a member of Penguin Group (USA) · NEW YORK

JEREMY P. TARCHER/PENGUIN
Published by the Penguin Group
Penguin Group (USA), 375 Hudson Street,
New York, New York 10014, USA

USA · Canada · UK · Ireland · Australia
New Zealand · India · South Africa · China

Penguin Books Ltd, Registered Offices: 80 Strand, London WC2R 0RL, England
For more information about the Penguin Group visit penguin.com

Most Tarcher/Penguin books are available at special quantity discounts for bulk purchase for sales promotions, premiums,
fund-raising, and educational needs. Special books or book excerpts also can be created to fit specific needs.
For details, write Penguin Group (USA) Special Markets, 375 Hudson Street, New York, NY 10014.

Library of Congress Cataloging-in-Publication Data

McCarty, Marietta, date.
The philosopher's table : how to start your philosophy dinner club—monthly
conversation, music, and recipes / Marietta McCarty.
p.   cm.
ISBN 978-1-58542-926-4
1. Philosophy—Miscellanea.   2. Dinners and dining.   I. Title.
BD31.M33   2013   2013009656
100—dc23

Printed in the United States of America
1   3   5   7   9   10   8   6   4   2

Book design by Gretchen Achilles

FOR MEL

MY TEACHER

Contents

INVITATION

1

THE JOY OF
SINGLE TASKING
January in Japan

5

MENTAL CLARITY
February in England

25

PERSISTENCE AND GRACE
March in Burma

47

COMMUNITY AND THE MELTING POT
April in Chicago

67

SIMPLE PLEASURES
May in Greece

89

LIBERATING EDUCATION
June in Brazil

107

SPIRITUAL HUNGER
July in Iraq

129

WHAT ABOUT LOVE?
August in Kentucky

149

A FRUITFUL
ECOLOGICAL SOLUTION
September in Kenya

169

RATIONAL DECISION MAKING
October in Germany

190

A SLOW DANCE WITH NATURE
November in China

209

DARE YOU
December in France

229

THANKSGIVING

251

The Philosopher's Table

Invitation

Dear Fellow Philosopher,

Please join me for dinner. Gather a few friends, old and new, perhaps a neighbor, maybe family members or colleagues. We're starting a philosophy supper group and making plans for a yearlong trip around the world

Here's a peek at the menu for twelve monthly evenings: lively conversation about universally intriguing issues, more knowledge of cultures near and far, genre-spanning music, and a feast of home cooking from Japan to France, Kentucky to Brazil. For years I've pulled up a chair at festive philosophers' tables just like the ones set for you in this book. Wherever I go, I find people thriving on hearty discussions. While telling stories, laughing, pondering, and questioning, diners develop a sense of belonging as they break bread, pass carafes, and wash dishes. Philosophy, music, and traditional cuisine spring from a particular culture while serving to define that culture, as well. Coming together in your homes, listening to the voices of your dinner partners, as well as those you'll meet from other times and places, you'll taste the hearts of Kenya and Greece, China and Iraq.

This book was an invigorating, joyful project for me to think about and to write. I chose the dinner topics after much thought, settling on the ones that continuously light conversational sparks. Yes, give me some persistence and grace. Hurry up with that mental clarity. Help wanted for decision making and adapting to change.

I worked with a head chef in creating and modifying dishes to match food and chapter themes in appealing combinations, and recipe testers and tweakers around the country prepared your meals and added their own just-right touches. The evenings you are about to share have been enjoyed in Pennsylvania, New Hampshire, California, Washington, Virginia, Massachusetts, Georgia, Vermont, and in my kitchen. Music lovers joined me in narrowing my picks, the decisions hotly contested after wonderfully long work. All the philosophers I looked to as representatives of their cultures are perennial favorites. When sorting through the suggestions given at the beginning and end of each chapter for your further exploration of that culture, I couldn't get enough. I wanted to learn more about a city, rain forest, museum, humanitarian, and an athlete.

As I wrote this book, I imagined countless, always-changing faces talking and eating around philosophy tables. Quite a treat to know that people speak face-to-face now, enjoying an exceptional kind of evening, feeding mind and body in comfortable companionship.

SOME KEY POINTS TO GET YOU STARTED

Whatever time of year your group is ready, whether August or December, start right there.

FOOD

• All recipes serve eight. Proportions and appetites will find each other.

• Allow plenty of time for this once-a-month happening. Though active preparation times are included for each dish, variations in pot and bowl sizes, stoves, knives, kitchen experience, etc., inevitably result in some deviation. (Do not worry—about anything!)

- Borrow whatever equipment you don't have on hand. Someone has that big pot, skillet, sieve, or large bowl. If not, improvise with confidence.

- Experiment with regional-ingredient substitutions, if you like. For example, root vegetables with similar densities are usually interchangeable.

- The chapters alternate between those offering recipes for two small plate dishes and others serving up three-recipe meals that always include dessert. We begin in January with small plates of good-luck New Year's noodles and chicken Yakitori, and conclude with December's three-course celebration, featuring Salmon Cooked on a Bed of Salt, Pot-au-Feu, and Clementine Soufflé.

- Tips are given for food and beverages that guests can contribute, and the person serving as host should delegate assignments freely and welcome surprises. All groups with which I'm familiar rotate hosting duties.

- Add individual touches: photographs of the release of Burmese political prisoners, the sights of Chicago, or your own travels to the night's featured location. Perhaps use that certain tablecloth and Grandmother's platters along with candles at a winter's table, or pull out those brightly colored quilts for the August picnic.

PHILOSOPHY

- Each chapter opens with my presentation of the topic and its importance. As you'll see, these topics sit on the tips of tongues, younger and older. Next, I introduce a philosopher whose work explores the issue in ways that have captivated my

3

companions in thought over the years. The philosopher's section comes in two parts, each described in one word, for good clarity and focus—first we look at the problem and then we find the solutions. For example, *stale* thinking about education is followed by *fresh* approaches.

- If you think you are a newcomer to philosophy, I doubt it. Whether we speak about these issues or not, they linger in our minds.

- Reward your group and yourself by reading that month's chapter in advance.

- I offer *one* topic for dinner conversation so that you can experience the satisfaction of a fully explored subject. Oh, yes, there will be times when everyone talks at once, the topic forgotten and memorable tangents enjoyed, and someone will call the group to attention again. And again. But don't worry about that. It's your night, after all.

MUSIC

- Collaborate on what works best for your group given the month's selections. Perhaps download the suggestions, maybe play your worn CDs of Dave Brubeck's jazz or Koko Taylor's blues, or raise another glass for vinyl recordings of Bill Monroe's bluegrass or compositions by Bach and Mozart.

- Of course feel free to bring your own irresistible tunes.

- Don't let the music interfere with conversation. Talk over it or turn it down. Many diners remember the evening as they enjoy the playlist afterward. (On the other hand, maybe consider letting the music take over for a while!)

The Joy of Single Tasking

JANUARY IN JAPAN

We all know people who glide through life as if sailing with the wind at their backs. An effortless style buoyed by humor, life gets lived with gusto. Meet my physician friend Marty, a hospital legend with good reason. No one can deny his enormous responsibilities to a horde of patients. I've watched him at work and play for years. Marty on the go treats each patient as an individual, stroking cheeks and answering questions as if hearing these worried queries for the first time. His steady presence and natural empathy spread down long hospital hallways, room by room, just as they lend calm at the nurse's station and on elevators. He deals swiftly and directly with incompetence and leaves the problem behind. Marty's consistently composed manner extends to his office staff and to the kiosk barista. He walks with no movement wasted, his step an unhurried giddyup. This laser focus is not limited to his professional life—favorite sports teams and leisure activities also win his riveted attention.

In all of my years of teaching and philosophy circling, no concept delights my companions more than what I call "single tasking." How alluring, the prospect of focusing on one thing at a time, doing that one thing well, and walking on. Our talk, however, soon turns to the surprising difficulty of putting this smart approach into practice. But Marty, along with many others in varying circumstances, proves that it can be done. Single tasking works—it increases efficiency, decreases stress, and maximizes our satisfaction in all of life's activities. What if Marty thought about all that lay before him, the known and possible unexpected twists, at the dawn of day? What would happen to his quick-stepping stride? Single tasking earns its place as the first topic in our book. If we are to progress to the second chapter, relish our conversations, remember to crank up the music and turn off the oven, then focusing on one thing at a time will make it all possible.

Listening intently at a philosophizing luncheon, Cliff, a participant, chose his words carefully. "I'm guessing that your emphasis on simply doing one thing at a time will be met with shouts of 'You're kidding!' It's the way I try to live, but most people brush the very notion off as unrealistic, maybe even lazy." My computer and I agree with Cliff's hunch. While *multitasking* passes the spell-check test, *single tasking* fails to qualify as one word. Yes, we make endless lists of things to do, unwittingly condition ourselves to take on too much, and succumb to the prevailing chaos of busyness. Saddled with anxiety, we can't catch our breath or catch up.

One example jostles itself to the forefront. Picture this. Teachers, parents, and volunteers sit around a table on the first day of a workshop devoted to sharing philosophy with children. A nice man, the last participant to arrive, pulls up a chair where his philosophy journal and pencil await. As introductions commence, he carefully positions his other supplies just so, at the ready: a cell phone, a small computer for Internet access, and his keys. He multitasks all morning . . . hasty conversation with now-distracted participants, clicked returns of messages, quick completion of his art and poetry assignments, and the occasional departure for a phone call or to move his car to another two-hour parking spot. It never occurred to him that his behavior was rude or that he was shortchanging his experience. After we talked privately at lunch and only the journal and pencil remained as his place setting, his attention and relaxation energized the room. He gave one hundred percent and everyone benefited from his eager, intelligent participation. Did he notice the change? Four days later, he looked ten years younger. As memory of the workshop dimmed, did he remember? I know that for me it was yet another lesson in the ease of the single task.

A fourth grader confided in me that she so wanted to become a writer but had no idea how to start. "How does anybody ever finish a *book*?" she wondered. I suggested that she take one very small thing to write about and focus only on that: every single thing about her birthday cake, or a tree on the playground, or her friend's face. I assured her that you can write only one word at a time and then a sentence appears . . . and one word at a time and then . . . a page! The process of writing a book models perfectly a single-tasked life. The exhilarating days given to the writing craft are for me the ones in which I am present only to that one exact spot where I am—searching for *this* one elusive word or massaging *that* one paragraph until its tension releases. If naughty thoughts lurch uninvited into my consciousness of the book in its entirety, writing stops and friends beware.

Fortunately, just as an author finds those words, we can jump off the chaos track. Abiding satisfaction comes to many new philosophers who commit to the process of gradually strengthening their mental discipline. We can build inner fortitude just as we train ourselves in other ways: practicing a musical instrument, hitting ball after ball with that bedeviling backhand, slowly exercising a weak knee back to healthy function. Savoring our lives, even though they are chock-full of responsibility and beset by some difficulty, strikes us as the wisest option. Having lots to do need not devolve into swirling busyness. Though the pace quickens, we can become more skilled at staying in the moment. As the child, the cashier, and the customer demand our attention in the grocery store, we stay right there with it all, poised and cash in hand. How? We practice concentration. Fully investing in our lives, being present now in *this* moment, proves the answer. Life is not a series of things to get done. Life is for living.

Our twelve evenings serve as the perfect manual for single tasking, offering the chance to soak up life's richness, moment by moment, with no goal beyond the time spent together. Paying attention to each ingredient as the whole dish bubbles to fruition requires the cook's undivided concentration—tasting the resulting flavors and picking up distinctive textures magnifies the diner's pleasure. Listening to music trains us to take special note of our lives, too. Hearing one instrument as well as the whole piece, picking up the resonance of both voice and guitar, and recognizing the sound of quiet spaces, all hone awareness. The repeated process of reading beforehand and absorbing the night's philosophical topic, then stepping back and allowing the ideas to take hold—this routine enhances alertness. Taking notice of the speaker's tone of voice, body movement, emotions, pauses, and breaths restores the disappearing art of conversation. Sucked in as undistracted listeners, we are present.

A joyous Zen Master from Japan tempts us with a timeless guarantee. Concentrating, doing one thing at a time, gives you a steely mind of your own. Your *own* steady mind returns. Shunryu Suzuki (shun-REE-oo suh-ZOO-kee) patiently reinforces our profound realization that we are here right now. Let's stay right here with him.

Prepping for Japan

Count poetic syllables with Bashō and Izumi Shikibu. . . . Watch Akira Kurosawa's *Ikiru*, Masayuki Suo's *Shall We Dance?*, and Kenji Mizoguchi's *The Life of Oharu*. . . . Round the bases with Sadaharu Oh, rooting for his Yomiuri Giants, and congratulate 2011 World Cup winning soccer stars Homare Sawa and Aya Miyama along with their coach Norio Sasaki. . . . Uncover the simple, calming rituals of the tea ceremony (*cha-no-yu*) as you take three and a half sips of tea in the style of Zen Tea Master Sen Rikyū. . . . Try your hand at the art of flower arranging (*ikebana*) and imagine Japanese ancient horseback archers (*yabusame*). . . . Discover the pioneering work of alternative farmer/philosopher Masanobu Fukuoka in *The One-Straw Revolution* and enter medieval court life through Sei Shōnagon's observations in *The Pillow Book*. . . . Listen closely to pianist and composer Joe Hisaishi's "View of Silence" and the tender piano tribute to Japan offered by Thelonious Monk in his "Kojo No Tsuki" ("Japanese Folk Song"). . . .

You must read each sentence with a fresh mind.

SHUNRYU SUZUKI,
Zen Mind, Beginner's Mind

Revved-up college students and car engines, plus the weight of nagging discontent and material possessions, greeted Suzuki upon his arrival in the sixties from Japan. Giving informal lectures at his Soto Zen monastery, on the outskirts of San Francisco, he sent many grateful pupils on their single-minded paths. Though reading one sentence, and then another, with a fresh mind poses a stiff challenge, we join our easygoing guru for a basic refresher course in his singularly focused technique. Concentrating and comprehending one sentence at one time—that's the goal. Game on.

LOST

"I lost my train of thought." How many times have you uttered this lament? How much simpler would life be if "one railway track thousands of miles long" (*Zen Mind*) described the mind's unswerving movement? Rookies join professional tennis players in their struggle to master the key to this game—keeping the eye on the ball. Help! Where is that one-track mind that can capture the smooth meeting of ball and strings? After some lessons with Suzuki, however, fewer balls ricochet off the racquet frame and bullet trains of thought glide uninterrupted along the track.

The same worry worn on the faces of his students still knits brows and freezes jaws today. Suzuki applauds that big first step taken by each of his students, the sincere acknowledgment that something isn't quite right . . . about me. No improvement can come to any life without the realization that there's life—and then there's me, somehow going against the grain. Honoring this off-kilter awareness that nips at my heels signals the beginnings of my effort to regain my touch.

Recently I was startled by a friend's bruised face and doubly swollen wrist. She had turned too sharply onto a road she'd driven countless times and careened into a ditch. Shaking her head in dismay, she swore, "I say it every day. I need to slow down and quit rushing through my life. Maybe now I will." Her sigh of "maybe now" speaks for all hopeful but stalling single taskers. How many times must Suzuki have thought about his students' recurring excuse of unavoidable busyness with an insightful sigh, that "If they say so, it is a sure sign they are spending their time in vain" (*Branching Streams Flow in the Darkness*)? Indeed, my frustrated friend listed all sorts of activities that she could drop that would free her to "do things that need to be done" (*Branching Streams*). Set in our ways, however, we fritter time away, flailing at our lives.

Doesn't this very basic predicament, one which we all share to some extent, ring true? While hands peel a banana, mind festers over a perceived slight. Words tumble out in conversation as mind wanders toward bike repair. Riding a steep mountain trail, the biker's helmet lies forgotten on the porch. The long anticipated evening disappoints, ruined by gnawing regret at its inevitable end, both parties guilty of "sacrificing this moment for the future" (*Branching Streams*). Body and mind divorce. Thinking and doing are separated. Is it as simple as the Master suggests? "Just make it clear where you are" (*To Shine One Corner of the World*) and things will get done more easily and more pleasantly. He quickly grew accustomed to outbursts of denial from his American students. They lived in the midst of a hectic world, while he enjoyed the retiring life of a Zen Buddhist monk. "Whatever you do, just do it" (*Not Always So*) was easy for him to say but completely unrealistic for them. Yet his advice to be where you are can work nicely for anyone determined to live more easily and fully. If we master time, our focus returns here and now, repairing this mind/body rift.

Let's slide next to Suzuki and, sitting on a wooden bench, listen closely to our tutorial. As children we existed in the present moment. With an attentive "beginner's mind" we listened to the story, followed the dandelion's fluff, observed the cat's sunlit shadow, and kicked the ball. Unfortunately and inevitably, the bustle of modern life rattles our minds and we lose this natural marriage of action and mind. We spin in an unreal loop, one foot cemented in worry about things neglected and the other foot hopping from item to item in a future to-do list. Frantic, we can't remember what was forgotten and we try to control what might happen. We want to finish everything at once yet nothing gets done. With too much going on, we pick up speed. "But the future is the future and the past is the past. This is our attitude and how we should live in this world. . . . If we do not forget this point, everything will be carried on beautifully" (*Zen Mind*). Since we *do* forget that only the present moment is real, though, we never stand or sit or act with purpose. Ironically, we waste time because we aren't present to spend it wisely. Too much zigzagging and too little composure!

The Zen Master's message sinks in. The noise of my fragmented mind bombards me with its jumble of fleeting ideas. As I play a losing game of mental hopscotch, the letter goes unwritten, the assignment remains incomplete, unwashed clothes pile high— conversations put off, promises broken, and kindness unnoticed. My stale, tired mind no longer distinguishes between what deserves my consideration and the much bigger "all" that does not belong to me. I take everything on and wear the load poorly. Like the pieces of an unsolved jigsaw puzzle, my mind is a mess.

But I get it. "Thinking which is divided is not true thinking. Concentration should be present . . ." (*Zen Mind*). Life is alive and I have a life to live. *Now* is the time.

FOUND

I accept the challenge of cultivating a steady state of mind and reclaiming my childlike "beginner's mind." I expect my attention to come and go, to be sharper some days more than others, and that's all right. I trust that stable focus will supplant more instinctively my customary waywardness.

Where to start? Where to end? How to settle myself? Suzuki's answer never changes. We must learn to sit. Five or ten (or more) minutes of sitting quietly, two or three times a day, can change lives dramatically. This simple act, requiring daily commitment, serves as the heart of a training regimen for increasing the power of concentration. The vitality resulting from sitting cannot be overstated. Sit where and as you are, nothing fancy, just sit. That's all? When I introduce my college students to Suzuki, I take them from the classroom to a campus garden. Awkward and uncertain at first, they leave books, phones, and backpacks behind. For some, the experience of sitting in silence on a hillside proves unnerving because the habit of multitasking goes unquestioned for so many of us. More than a few new philosophers admit initial panicky responses to the stillness: "Did I replace the gas cap on my truck? Why am I sitting here when I have so much to do?" I can imagine more: "Did *she* lock the door to keep our belongings safe? What is *she* thinking? Who *hired* her?" Yet, how often these same students share their appreciation at semester's end that it was during these days of garden serenity that they learned the most about the course, about themselves, about life.

The better concentrated sitter expects the coming and welcomes the going of restlessness and aggravation. Trusting the rewards of practiced focus, our discipline improves. Single-minded seeds take secure root and flourish with time. If we ignore the prevailing penchant for the quick fix and give ourselves a chance, this soothing repetition of sitting and breathing, inhaling and exhaling, seeps into our lives as we tend to animals at the emergency clinic, parent an angry child, or participate in a meeting marred by discord. My philosophical partners of all ages marvel at the ease granted by single mindedness once they taste it. I watch children eager to close their eyes and sit silently at the beginning of class. "It makes me smarter." "I forget why I was mad." When I join dinner groups assembling at the end of the work day, the outstretched-legged leisure of a few minutes of silence disperses cares.

Ah. Stepping back and taking stock of my life, I freely set limits now. With time to think, I let some things go and give others their deserved priority. Contented and perhaps a bit surprised, I discover that with fewer things competing for my attention, I beam direct focus on the task at hand. Missions accomplished. As time lets loose its stranglehold, I delight that more time appears for my efficient use. What a relief to make time work for me. Each activity I do, question I ask, scene I contemplate, or commitment I make gathers me in, totally involved. An everyday sincerity marks my moves and my stillness. New "sitters" offer examples of the joys of single tasking. "When I prepare a meal, it's as if I'm serving my heart on a platter." "Running without headphones relaxes me." "I'm an alert driver now." My favorite: "Trust me. I'm a much better kisser."

"Just continue in your calm, ordinary practice and your character will be built up" (*Zen Mind*). Here are a few suggestions, popular with my students, for your daily practice in fully concentrated living: Find a one-word description that best fits an emotion, a situation, or a relationship. Watch nothing but the ball at a sporting event, now focus on just one player, and finally, fasten your gaze only on the referee. Rake leaves. Clean the house with no electronic accompaniment. Consciously feel the keys of the laptop, smell the scent of rain, distinguish between shades of gray, tune in to the pitch of the catbird's cry. Reel in the wandering mind, best done with a smile.

More and more, you are living your one life, at last experiencing the breath-giving union between activity and mind. "You understand; you have full understanding within yourself. There is no problem" (*Zen Mind*).

Runners take your mark. . . . Get set. . . . Sit.

AND YOUR TOPIC FOR DINNER CONVERSATION IS

"If you're alert, you can hear the tide turn" (*To Shine One Corner*). When have you experienced this intensity of focus? Describe the feeling of single tasking. Do you want to bring such attentiveness to your daily life? If you find this an attractive proposition, how can you slowly build good concentration, moment by moment, doing one thing at a time? Be practical and one-pointedly specific about *your* life.

THE DOORBELL RINGS

Guests will want to contribute their own favorite Japanese small plates to the evening's menu. Purchasing sushi, seaweed salad, or miso soup provides an easy way to sample the clean flavors of Suzuki's country. Grocery versions of flavored rice crackers (*senbei*), traditionally baked over a wood fire, can be served with a topping of your choice. Invite diners to bring precut "ribbons" of their favorite root vegetables to include in tonight's soba noodle recipe. Sake, warm or slightly chilled, and traditional Japanese beer provide refreshing liquid accompaniments. The slow, painstaking art of sake brewing in Japan yields complex flavors— some of the finest sake produced in Japan today originates from one-hundred-year-old water that began as rain or snow at the mountaintop and made its determined, slow descent. Traditional desserts usually consist of fresh seasonal fruits, such as apples from the Fuji region, fresh or dried persimmons, and green tea (*matcha*) ice cream. All make fine pickups for evening's end.

Travel in the sixties with the Dave Brubeck Quartet and listen to American *Jazz Impressions of Japan*, especially the lovely "Koto Song." As you gather in the kitchen, swing your hips with Akiko Tsuruga and "Take It Easy" as you taste her "Frim Fram Sauce." Move your feet to Takuya Kuroda's soulful trumpet tribute to a surprising appetizer, the "Blue Tomato." As you settle in for your discussion of single tasking, let Midori's violin guide you with her *Encore!*

Mitsuko Uchida's legendary interpretations of Western classical music serve as a model of single tasking. Imagine the concentration required to enter the soul of a piano concerto by Mozart and make the piece belong both to him and to her. Listen to Uchida play and direct the Cleveland Orchestra in Mozart's concertos nos. 20 and 27. Play *and* direct! She sets the perfect pitch for good conversation. Conductor Seiji Ozawa and his very own Saito Kinen Orchestra walk you down composer Toru Takemitsu's *November Steps*. Hear the timbre and almost touch the texture of the lute (*biwa*) and the bamboo flute (*shakuhachi*). Switching the tempo, the piano and vibraphone duo of Makoto Ozone and Gary Burton gently merges genres with jazz improvisations of classical *Virtuosi*.

As you finish your group discussion, linger over thoughts of "The Good Life" hinted at by the bouncy organ played by Atsuko Hashimoto. Serve your guests green tea in humble vessels that honor the simplicity of the Japanese tea ceremony. Say farewell with Hiromi Uehara's "Love and Laughter" and bounce into the night with her piano *Spiral* at your back.

In the Kitchen

DASHI

Bring your beginner's mind into the kitchen as you assemble the building blocks for this meal of traditional Japanese favorites. The ingredient lineup in these dishes yields simple tastes of culinary focus and clarity. Each of the following recipes combines dashi, an easily produced Japanese stock made with dried seaweed and bonito flakes, with familiar Japanese flavorings such as soy sauce and mirin. Inhale the aromas and enjoy the pared-down textures of food that goes down well with Suzuki's teachings.

PREPARATION. 30 minutes (5 minutes active)
YIELD: approximately 2½ quarts (enough for both noodle and yakitori recipes)

2 pieces of dried kombu (seaweed), 4 inches long

2½ quarts cold water

1½ cups shaved, dried bonito flakes (made from smoked bonito fish)

1. In a large pot, soak the kombu in 2½ quarts of cold water for 5–10 minutes. Bring the mixture to a boil over medium-high heat.

2. Once boiling, immediately turn off the heat and discard the kombu. Stir in the bonito flakes and let steep for 3–4 minutes (increase this time if you prefer a smokier, fishier flavor).

3. Strain through a fine sieve.

HOT SOBA NOODLES WITH DAIKON RADISH AND EDAMAME

Observe each nutty strand of these traditional Japanese buckwheat noodles with the same focus bestowed on the morning glory vine by eighteenth-century haiku master and Buddhist nun Chiyo-ni: "of a single, long vine / one hundred opening lives" (*Women in Praise of the Sacred*). Soba noodles, sometimes called "year-end noodles," are often eaten to celebrate a fresh start for a new year. This recipe allows for 2 ounces of dried soba noodles and 1 cup of broth per guest. Depending upon the size of your bowls (and appetites), you may adjust accordingly.

PREPARATION: 1 hour

¼ cup mirin (Japanese cooking wine)[1]

¼ cup packed light brown sugar

1¼ cups soy sauce

2 quarts dashi[2] (see master recipe, and be sure to save remainder for yakitori)

2 packages dry soba noodles (1 pound total)

1 daikon radish (a large, white, carrot-shaped root vegetable known for its peppery taste), or 1 bunch of conventional radishes (and any ribbons of favorite root vegetables supplied by guests)

6 ounces frozen, shelled edamame

1. To prepare the broth, bring the mirin to a boil in a large saucepan. Add the light brown sugar and stir until dissolved, then

---

1. Mirin can be replaced in this recipe with 3 tablespoons sake and 1 tablespoon sugar.

2. You can substitute low-sodium fish broth for dashi.

add the soy sauce and dashi. Heat the mixture, stirring until hot. Remove from the heat.

2. Bring a large pot of water to a boil (amount may be specified on the soba noodle package) and add the noodles. Immediately lower the heat so that the water is at a simmer, not a full boil. Cook 7–8 minutes, or according to package directions. Noodles should be cooked through, but not overcooked. Drain and rinse the soba noodles under cold water, to remove the excess starch, until the water runs clear.

3. Use a vegetable peeler to shave the daikon radish into long ribbons. (If using conventional radishes, grate or cut into thin slices.) Place in a small serving bowl, along with any root vegetable ribbons supplied by guests, and set aside.

4. Prepare the edamame according to the package directions. Place in a small serving bowl and set aside.

5. Slowly reheat the broth. Add the noodles and heat until just warm. Ladle into individual bowls and serve with the reserved radish and edamame.

YAKITORI

Traditional Japanese homes centered around *irori*, square fire pits built into the floor, designed for grilling. Today yakitori, or "grilled bird," is a popular item sold in food stalls throughout Japan. Although Zen Master Suzuki was primarily vegetarian, he did not insist on any strict food regimen outside the monastery and cautioned his students against postures of moral superiority because "you have to kill vegetables too" (*Crooked Cucumber*). Gathered around your flame, watch as these bite-size morsels acquire their trademark caramelized char.

PREPARATION: 2 hours (45 minutes active)

16–24 bamboo skewers (2 or 3 skewers per person)

2 pounds skinless, boneless chicken thighs, cut into 1-inch pieces

2 cups sake

2 cups soy sauce

¾ cup mirin

½ cup packed light brown sugar

1½ cups dashi (reserved from master recipe) or water

3 tablespoons vegetable oil, and more if needed

You may want to create your own backyard yakitori stall by following Japanese grill expert Tadashi Ono's foil-covered-brick grilling method. He wraps two to four bricks in heavy-duty aluminum foil and places them vertically on either side of the grill grate. Arranging the chicken skewers so they span the foil-covered bricks keeps your skewers from burning but allows the chicken to brown nicely.

1. Soak the bamboo skewers in water for at least 30 minutes. Drain. Spear 2–3 pieces of chicken on each skewer.

2. In a medium saucepan, add the sake, soy sauce, mirin, brown sugar, and dashi to make the marinade. Bring to a boil and cook until slightly thickened, 30–45 minutes. Set aside 1 cup of the marinade to use as a dipping sauce.

3. Prepare a grill or heat a heavy skillet over high heat. Brush the chicken skewers with the oil. Cook for 3 minutes on each side. Baste with the marinade and continue to grill about 2 minutes per side, or until the chicken is golden brown and firm. If you are using a skillet, you will need to cook the chicken in batches.

4. Serve with the reserved marinade for dipping.

JAPAN TO GO

Read Haruki Murakami's *What I Talk About When I Talk About Running* and Kenzaburo Oe's *Teach Us to Outgrow Our Madness*. . . . Appreciate Shigeru Ban's architectural innovation as well as the firm Atelier Bow-Wow. . . . Dress warmly for a February trip to Sapporo on the island of Hokkaido for its Snow Festival of ice sculptures, followed, when April arrives, with a walk along the stone trail of the Philosopher's Path as the cherry blossoms fall in Kyoto. . . . Tune into a contemporary beat, staying up late for "Tokyo Nights" with Puffy AmiYumi and agreeing with Kazuki Tomokawa to "Say with Conviction, I Am Alive" in this moment. . . . Slow down with a listen to Bach Collegium Japan complemented by a poem from Gensei or Issa. . . . Check out a performance by world champion gymnast Kohei Uchimura and creations by famed polka-dot artist Yayoi Kusama. . . . Focus on director Yasujiro Ozu's concentrated "tatami shot" showcased in his *Noriko* trilogy, imitate the methodical artistry of origami master Akiri Yoshizawa in Vanessa Gould's documentary *Between the Folds*, and savor director David Gelb's feast as *Jiro Dreams of Sushi*. . . .

RESOURCES

PHILOSOPHY

Zen Mind, Beginner's Mind by Shunryu Suzuki.

Branching Streams Flow in the Darkness by Shunryu Suzuki, edited by Mel Weitsman and Michael Wenger.

To Shine One Corner of the World by Shunryu Suzuki, edited by David Chadwick.

Not Always So by Shunryu Suzuki, edited by Edward Espe Brown.

MUSIC

Jazz Impressions of Japan by the Dave Brubeck Quartet: "Koto Song."

Oriental Express by Akiko Tsuruga: "Take it Easy," "Frim Fram Sauce."

Bitter & High by Takuya Kuroda: "Blue Tomato."

Midori Encore! by Midori.

Mozart Piano Concertos Nos. 20 K.466 & 27 K.595 by Wolfgang Amadeus Mozart, Cleveland Orchestra, Mitsuko Uchida, conducting and piano.

Takemitsu: November Steps; Eclipse; Viola Concerto by Toru Takemitsu, Saito Kinen Orchestra, Seiji Ozawa, conducting: "November Steps."

Virtuosi by Gary Burton and Makoto Ozone.

Until the Sun Comes Up by Atsuko Hashimoto: "The Good Life."

Spiral by Hiromi Uehara: "Love and Laughter," "Spiral."

FOOD

Rediscovering Rikyu and the Beginnings of the Japanese Tea Ceremony by Herbert E. Plutschow.

Women in Praise of the Sacred: 43 Centuries of Spiritual Poetry by Women, edited by Jane Hirshfield: "Morning Glory" by Chiyo-ni.

Just Hungry (blog) by Makiko Itoh, 2003. justhungry.com

Crooked Cucumber: The Life and Zen Teaching of Shunryu Suzuki by David Chadwick.

Japanese Food Report (blog) by Harris Salat, 2007. japanesefoodreport.com

The Japanese Grill: From Classic Yakitori to Steak, Seafood, and Vegetables by Tadashi Ono and Harris Salat.

Mental Clarity

FEBRUARY IN ENGLAND

Opening night arrived. Greeting college students at the classroom door for the first time, I was excited and unsure. Who are they? What do they expect from an introductory course in philosophy? Are they tired at day's end? Will they stay for the full three hours? Have they picked up on my rookie status? With a deep breath, the lecture began: "'Philosophy' literally means 'love of wisdom,' a word that. . . ." Boom! Slapping his desk with one hand and raising the other hand high, a man (whom I would get to know quite well) exclaimed from the back row: "Lady! You have confused me." I would never be more startled in the classroom. "Well, it didn't take long, did it?" I replied. Unwinding with a burst of group laughter that often accompanies philosophizing, we were off.

Though I still think he could have given me a little more time, I understood exactly why my student banged his desk. Whenever I think about the formal definition of philosophy, I also find it lacking. What a flat and disappointing phrase for an electric and lifelong, personal and social activity. This hardworking man wanted an entertaining, practical, and beneficial course. I returned to the next class with my homemade description of philosophy: "the art of clear thinking." This definition resonates with students of all ages, from wildly divergent backgrounds, and in all kinds of settings. Three slaps on the desk for mental clarity!

I relish the opportunity to make a case for the value of philosophy. Its appeal stirred unconsciously in my childhood and its benefits explain my choice of profession. Philosophy's rewards gently saturate each day. What a joy to watch reflection and conversation enhance my students' lives in innumerable ways. Here's my story, theirs, and now yours.

I remember me like yesterday, a girl having fun and earning college credits for doing something natural and fulfilling. Childhood wonder recharging and curiosity spiraling, I look out the window and at the instructor, back and forth, my mind buzzing. Philosophy is my ticket to travel the world through minds from other cultures and times. What an unfathomable world and how pleasurable its investigation. Haze lifts, strips of gauze pull back, and I can think about—anything. Increasing mental clarity serves me well in tennis matches, in determining how to spend my time, and in correcting nonstop mistakes. Questions outweigh answers, serving as motivation to step out of my own way and let the world fire my imagination. Life exposes itself and I feel inexplicably alive. One lucky girl. . . . Much of this I realize in retrospect. After my academic study ended, ten years passed. Ideas, discussions, and readings simmered and took on fresh meaning. Philosophy accompanied me everywhere, adapting smoothly to the changes in my life. Then, on opening night, I threw my first pitch.

Philosophy's gift is the possession of mental clarity. What is clear thinking? Mental clarity is a no-nonsense way of understanding the world as it is. A razor-sharp mind weeds out what is irrelevant and off track, cutting to life's core, prying it open with inquisitiveness. Shaping such a mind takes work. Just as a concert oboist and a chef in training diligently hone their skills, mental clarity requires similar daily maintenance. Missteps are inevitable: prejudging situations and people, reacting without thinking, falling under anger's sway. Recognizing confusion when it rears up becomes easier, though, and vigilance pays off. Practicing clear thinking readies the mind—for everything.

Empty space takes up the most room in a clear mind. At the outset, philosophical introspection and discussion often reveal a largely unexamined life. Clutter of all kinds jumbles the mind. "Why did I think that was wrong?" "Why would I use such language?" "How could I choose this path?" When we clear away the debris of unfounded opinions and careless assumptions, room for straightforward thinking increases. Unlearning cleanses the mind and creates space for new ideas. Like a fresh breeze, wonder blows through the ears. The world appears more transparent, less confusing. Purity graces thought.

Do I know *for sure* that philosophy works? Why discuss ethical issues, personal responsibility, decision making, justice, or joy? Testimony to mental clarity from my companions over the years shouts a loud "yes." Whether a child philosopher, college student, reader, member of a philosophy club or dinner group, I have been privy to the sometimes dramatic, more often gradual transformations induced by the art of clear thinking. How I admire the everyday philosopher's skill set, the unique ways in which an individual uses new ideas (or the reminder of old but forgotten insights) to cope with hardship, alter course, or embrace a chance. Through philosophical dialogue, participants become more articulate, aware of the power of language, and therefore more sensitive in their choice of words. Clarity improves with every sentence, spoken and written. Confidence and creativity perk up. Ironically, budding philosophers go easier on themselves while also setting higher expectations. Looser shoulders shrug off a sense of entitlement and the wearying bent for argument. Flexibility wins, rigidity loses, and success and hardship are both juggled masterfully. We get to know the people at our dinner tables *as well as* ourselves. As we plant trees with Wangari Maathai in modern Kenya and stroll with Lao Tzu in ancient China, the world shrinks and expands. An ethic of compassion blossoms as gratitude for life's bounty warms diners' hearts. Paradoxes that accompany mental clarity exhilarate its beneficiaries: "I dig solitude and conversation." "Sometimes, when I think hard and long, I start laughing." "I take myself more but less seriously." "Even though I'm now aware of social problems and my own hangups, I'm more hopeful."

Philosophy's well of clarity has staying power, there to draw from as needed. Like ointment stashed away just in case, it binds wounds and steadies unrest. One of my most profound philosophical experiences occurred not long ago, serving as a vivid reminder of the effort required to keep one's eye on the prize of clear thinking. I was scooped up by surprise—my week devoted to a down-to-the-last-detail final proof of my manuscript suddenly coincided with giving a scheduled speech some hours away and my mother's unexpected weeklong hospital stay. Three towns, many animals, plenty of worry, no way out. But the first night, while I was sitting in the hospital, philosophy worked its magic. As I carefully reread the manuscript, peace and a way through—not a way out—surfaced. I learned about simplicity, perspective, and serenity from someone I didn't know! Add nothing, neither anxiety nor projection, to the situation. Step back, take the long view, step back in. Move *with* events, one at a time. Pay attention to people in hallways and elevators who also have someone they love in the hospital. Express gratitude for generosity. Know the difference between things in my control and things that are not. It worked.

Now our dinner group sets sail for England. I can imagine no better personal trainer in philosophy than Bertrand Russell. Provocative and humorous, he takes the pain out of mental muscle building. As the mind lifts philosophical weights, growing stronger, the heart opens wide. Power up—barbells rising.

PREPPING FOR ENGLAND

Listen to the news on the BBC, music by Adele and Coldplay, Michael Kiwanuka and Laura Marling, and to your guide at the British Museum. . . . Go punting down the river Thames, leisurely viewing the heart of London, and stop for a village stay in the rolling hills of the Cotswolds. . . . Break the four-minute mile alongside Roger Bannister, win the London Marathon with Paula Radcliffe, and swing your mallet in a game of croquet. . . . Appreciate the pooling of English talent in the 1972 and 2007 film versions of *Sleuth*, rent a cottage in the mountainous Lake District, play with Beatrix Potter and J. K. Rowling, and soak in the ambience of Royal Albert Hall with Harrison's friends in a *Concert for George*. . . . Take in a Harold Pinter and a Noël Coward play, talk with soccer fans in Tottenham or Manchester, read a short story by each of the sisters A. S. Byatt and Margaret Drabble, grab a seat at Lord's Cricket Ground, and recite John Keats's "Ode on a Grecian Urn." . . .

THERE ARE THOSE WHO THINK THAT CLARITY, BECAUSE IT IS DIFFICULT AND RARE, SHOULD BE SUSPECT. THE REJECTION OF THIS VIEW HAS BEEN THE DEEPEST IMPULSE OF MY PHILOSOPHICAL WORK.

BERTRAND RUSSELL, Preface, *The Basic Writings of Bertrand Russell*

Bertrand Russell's passion for philosophy entices many to become lovers of wisdom.

He never doubts philosophy's value for the contemplative individual or sets a limit on what the thinker can bring to the world. He lived long, protesting two World Wars and the buildup of nuclear arsenals, peddling mental clarity as the cure for the world's ills. Winner of a Nobel Prize and a world traveler whose hometown was the universe, Russell invites you home for dinner. He prepares his specialty, a heaping platter of "goods of the mind."

CLOUDY

"I'm not a carpet, I'm a thinking person." "My mind is sending me places I shouldn't be going . . . can't tell you where." "Philosophy blows my mind open when it vacuums my head." Thus speak the child philosophers! They make quick pals with Russell, trusting that by growing into clear thinkers, their days will be "filled with life and hope and joy" ("Principles of Social Reconstruc- tion," *Basic Writings*). The full-throttled whirl of childhood rarely follows adults into later years. Where do the questions go? What happens to that relentless "But why?" Who puts the damper on fantasy and adventure?

Gobbled up by a big and sometimes in- timidating world, we let insecurity wiggle into our psyches. Russell introduces us to the "practical man," jailed by his or her anx- ieties. Knowing only one way of life, edu- cated that "my" country, "my" religion, and "my" politics are right, I hunker down. Dif- ferences and the faintest tug of uncertainty upset me. I reduce the universe to the small world of my private concerns and beliefs. I tuck my mind away, feeding it only a steady dose of me, avoiding uncertainty. Stand back. Stop the press. Close the books. Watch out, Russell warns. Such insecurity spawns the twin demons of fear and ar- rogance, trapping anyone in its clutches, corralling the mind into a seemingly safe cage. Let's deal straight up with fear and ar- rogance so that "the prison walls of the commonplace are broken down" ("Social Reconstruction," *Basic Writings*). Forward, ho!

Fear produces the herd instinct. If you're not in my manufactured tribe, lock down. This crowd mentality lurks everywhere. In graduate school, I observed faculty members lunching only with likeminded colleagues. Sharing philosophy with children, parents occasionally expressed outrage at "these crazy ideas they are talking about with you," which included such topics as bullying, courage, compassion, and justice. The possibility that their child might reach beyond the parents' known world fueled fear-based anger. Sad college students withdrew from classes, unable to resist their partners' disapproval of the "change" in their interests. We surround ourselves with people who share our views, lifestyles, and future plans, thereby ensuring that the world shrinks to our (dis)comfort zones. This ruinous bargain comes at a steep price—the shortchanging of our humanity. We choose false security over intellectual and emotional freedom, and this "habit of passive acceptance is a disastrous one" ("Social Reconstruction," *Basic Writings*).

Having lost all appreciation for "goods of the mind," this far from "practical man" declines all mental stimulation. Ignorance beats a free-ranging intellect. Philosophy circles rumble with proofs of Russell's conviction that "fear makes man unwise" ("Portraits from Memory," *Basic Writings*), tales told of time wasted stuck in paralyzing negativity, intentionally hurting others, alienating intimates and passersby . . . "I was afraid of who I was, who I could be, and who I wasn't." "I remember crying as a kid when I heard there was more than one religion." "I can't let myself go—I'm uncomfortable in my body much less my mind." Russell helps us laugh at ourselves by adding that "sex education frequently produces nervous disorders" ("Education and the Social Order," *Basic Writings*).

We soldier on. Choosing to "wear an armor designed to conceal the frightened child within" ("Portraits from Memory," *Basic Writings*), the practical man and woman hide behind the swagger of arrogance. Voices vie at dinner tables to offer examples of insecurity's second offspring, empty pride. "I don't play golf on public courses." "Why would a secretary campaign for school board?" "That lowbrow music, such tacky furniture, those uneducated shop owners. . . ." Our strutting masks insecurity about . . . what exactly? Hold it. I think maybe my boasting stems from knowing how much I don't know and that I lack any basis for my most cherished opinions. Under the rule of fear and ego, I haven't been smart. I held back from intimacy, used sarcasm to put people off, wallowed in the shallow waters of self-absorption. Repressed by insecurity, I painted a distorted, untrue picture of the world and its inhabitants. "The outer world is bleak, the inner world is stuffy. This is not how human relations should be. They should be free and spontaneous" ("Life Without Fear," *Basic Writings*). The fog lifts a bit.

How embarrassing, my self-righteousness, "right" about what? I've never thought for myself—there, I said it! "The first step in wisdom . . . is to open the windows of the ego as wide as possible" ("If We Are to Survive This Dark Time," *Basic Writings*).

Russell cheers on his mates. By lifting the weights of fear and arrogance, the heavy clouds of self-absorption slowly but surely give way to mental clarity. He rewards our labor with an offer of a new way of seeing, the proposition of looking at the world from the viewpoint of the "not-self." Seeing the world not as myself, not full of myself. . . . Using an*other* perspective promises relief, thrills, and unlimited opportunity. Leapfrogging over myself, I jump unafraid into the world.

SUNNY

Greet my student Justin, a once self-described "practical man," standing in for the practical man in all of us. A father of two, studying multicultural ethical perspectives upon returning to school after losing his job, staying at home while his wife works, his self-esteem already shaken *before* philosophy, Justin admits: "I've been afraid of what people think and I'm feeling a failure. Now I question everything. Why I think there's some role I should be playing, my parenting approach, my language, many of the positions taken by my church . . . my whole life is up in the air . . . and I love it." Every morning I heard the patter of his quick feet coming down the hall, excitedly bringing yet another news item to share with me and the class. Fear's departure leaves room for philosophy to do its thing.

A new viewfinder delivers clarity—the lens of the not-self frees thinkers with a surge of life's blood. The not-self prods us gently, presenting us with a more objective, true vision of the world. Are you ready for a Russell workout? Try sinking into your best self, the not-self. Let the world be, without imposing any preconceptions on it. Imagine past ages: drawings on cave walls, the Ice Age, seismic geologic shifts, sails fluttering in uncharted seas, stained glass, and the changes wrought by inventions such as the printing press and the sewing machine. Look up: mentally exiting this cosmos, entertaining the idea of other universes, floating beyond comprehension into mystery, What else. . . . Look down: your feet stand on a spinning world. How many feet balance on this one perch? Oh, the infinite variety of life stories told before and after yours, the myriad lives complementing your life right now. Anticipate future ages: contemplate how those standing in your place might recall your time here now. Breathe in the fresh air of the "many questions that must remain insoluble to the human intellect," feasting on "the uncertainty of philosophy" (*The Problems of Philosophy*). Experience the dizzying possibilities that humility affords, self-absorption dissolving in amazement. Intellectual fervor is its own reward.

The stars come out. Diners delight. "Only when I stop thinking about myself can I think clearly." "Clarity does not come from certainty. What a relief." "Saying 'I don't know' marks the beginning of my knowing." Cloudburst! Simple modesty hands me "the philosophic life . . . calm and free" (*The Problems of Philosophy*). What a world and, oh, this brand-new not-me. . . .

Faces emerge. An NPR host bids me farewell after our interview, returning to her daily routine of listening to broadcasts at complete odds with hers—in content, tone, and purpose. How wise to "seek out people with whom you disagree" ("Unpopular Essays," *Basic Writings*). I repeatedly watch a diet of goods of the mind open closed hearts of the disgruntled diner, hurt child, and lonely college student as "the vexations of daily life come to feel trivial" ("Adventures of the Mind," *Basic Writings*). Trouble ahead, I sense, as I see a question form on a man's pursed lips. Perched on the edge of his seat in the front row of the audience at a literary festival, he volleys my way: "When I told my wife I was coming to your talk, she said philosophy was a bunch of '$#!@#!&*.' What would you say to her?" (I would *not* say that I'm thinking that this is *your* opinion!) I *would* say something like: Please tell your wife that her language is very colorful. Also: A life without mental clarity is too small and too hard. Without light in our minds, how can we communicate and solder relationships, experience joy and deal with sorrow, appreciate our place in nature, or love life? If I'm fuzzy about the meaning of happiness, where will my priorities lead? Shouldn't I contemplate what goodness means? If I think only about myself, can I ever know you, or anyone? If I don't explore the world, I'll miss out on some kind of miracle—every day.

Count on this: "Philosophy does not cease to suggest and inspire a way of life" (*A History of Western Philosophy*). How can you be proud of your mind? How would you live? My college student Leon resolved "to go through life with my hand raised and a question ready." Mental clarity rubs off on every life it touches. If the contagion spreads, anything is possible. What if we were all free "citizens of the universe" (*The Problems of Philosophy*)? What about *that* life?

Our work always waits for us. We live in foggy times, just as Russell did. "Until we have set our own house in order, I think that we had better leave the moon in peace" ("The Expanding Mental Universe," *Basic Writings*). But we can look up.

AND YOUR TOPIC FOR DINNER CONVERSATION IS

"We have to learn to think in a new way" ("Portraits from Memory," *Basic Writings*). Describe some old ways of thinking that you want to discard. How will you think in a "new way"? Give specific examples. In what ways will your mental renaissance affect your life? Russell insists that your newfound clarity will affect others, as well. Do you agree? Explain.

THE DOORBELL RINGS

There's no question that "ale's the stuff to drink" on an evening in England. Guests can tote their favorite or first-time English ale or dark porter beers. The artist Hogarth may have been on to something when he depicted a healthy, beer-drinking society in *Beer Street*, which stands in bold contrast to the slovenly inhabitants portrayed in his companion print, *Gin Lane*. Strong cheese matches well with strong beer—Britain's famed blue-veined Stilton is often called the

King of Cheeses. Stilton and water crackers pair well.

"Come All Ye," the folk rockers of Fairport Convention welcome fellow "rolling minstrels," warming the room with traditional sounds of the British Isles. Mandolins and fiddles incite diners to "rouse the spirit of the earth." Inimitable guitarist Eric Clapton shows up completely *Unplugged*, sporting "Layla" on one arm and "Alberta" on the other. "Hey Hey," Eric! Claire Martin's jazz vocals live up to her album's title: *A Modern Art*. Kick back with her in "lowercase" and "Nirvana," ah "So Twentieth Century." The Beatles offer two tunes to lure you into your discussion of mental clarity. "Across the Universe" you go, aware that "Tomorrow Never Knows."

As you gather for conversation, settle in with vocalist Cleo Laine and her husband and bandleader, musician and arranger Johnny Dankworth. Their jazzy/classical *Collection* makes "Stormy Weather" desirable and lends rhythmic voice to a number of Shakespearean sonnets. "If Music Be the Food of Love," eat up and "play on." The tender strumming of John McLaughlin's guitar ripens the mood for conversation with his *Time Remembered*. A grownup boy from Liverpool composed a classical piece sure to enhance mental clarity. Paul McCartney's *Ocean's Kingdom* moves and calms, a work commissioned and performed by the New York City Ballet. Keep "Movement 1: Ocean's Kingdom," in the background as dialogue peaks and winds down. Look out a window, stretching to "Movement 4: Moonrise."

Elvis Costello picks up the pace with his rendition of countryman Nick Lowe's "(What's So Funny 'bout) Peace, Love, and Understanding." Surprise! A Detroit songstress chock-full of soul rocks the house with her *Interpretations* of the Beatles and Steve Winwood, the Animals and Led Zeppelin, those Rolling Stones and the Moody Blues, Derek and the Dominos and Elton

John. All the blokes! Bettye LaVette makes their music hers, and yours, while giving familiar tunes emotive newness. Each person gets to pick an original to play before or after listening to her version. My turn! LaVette and the Who swap versions of Pete Townshend's "Love Reign O'er Me." Bask in the music as the steam rises from your cup of Earl Grey tea. Fairport Convention bids you a fond "Farewell, Farewell."

In the Kitchen

ZESTY ARTICHOKE DIP

The artichoke thistle was a relative newcomer to the aristocratic table, first appearing in England in Henry VIII's garden in the early sixteenth century. Despite its prickly exterior, the artichoke found a devoted following in the reserved and usually guarded Brits. A sought-after and, at times, thorny dinner party guest himself, Russell faithfully arrived with a feisty intellect and quick wit.

PREPARATION: 1 hour (15 minutes active)

8 ounces cream cheese, at room temperature

8 ounces mascarpone cheese, at room temperature

2–3 teaspoons minced garlic

⅓ cup grated Parmesan cheese, preferably Parmigiano Reggiano

2 tablespoons heavy cream

1 tablespoon fresh lemon juice

1 teaspoon cayenne pepper, or to taste

1 teaspoon salt

1 teaspoon black pepper

1½ cups thoroughly drained and coarsely chopped canned artichoke hearts (packed in water)

Melba toast, for serving

1. Preheat the oven to 275 degrees.

2. Using a wooden spoon, blend the cream cheese and mascarpone cheese in a medium bowl. Add the remaining ingredients, except the artichoke hearts, and stir until well blended. Mix in the artichoke hearts.

3. Spread the mixture in a medium-sized shallow dish and bake for 45 minutes, or until bubbly and brown. Serve hot on Melba toast.

STOUT BEEF WITH BISCUITS

Ever since Neolithic-era farmers in Britain discovered that simmering meat in water at the fire's edge yielded a more tender roast, English cooks have exhibited affection for slow-cooked stews. From the Sunday "joint" celebrated in Henry Fielding's eighteenth-century patriotic ballad, "The Roast Beef of Old England," to pub favorites such as meat pie and Yorkshire pudding, evidence of an enduring love of beef (and beer) abounds in England. This braised beef classic topped with biscuits features tender morsels of beef cooked slowly in the bitter, caramel flavors of stout.

PREPARATION: 3 hours, 45 minutes (1 hour active)

STOUT BEEF

2 tablespoons butter

1 tablespoon olive oil, plus additional as needed for browning beef

4 ounces pancetta or lean bacon, ¼-inch thick, diced

3 pounds chuck stew beef, cut into generous 1½-inch pieces

½ cup all-purpose flour

1½ cups coarsely chopped red onions

2 tablespoons Worcestershire sauce

6 medium carrots, peeled and cut into 2-inch-long rounds

3 celery stalks, cut into 1-inch-long pieces

3 cups stout

1½ cups beef or chicken stock

2 bay leaves

1 teaspoon dried rosemary

1 teaspoon salt

1 teaspoon freshly ground pepper

12 ounces fresh mushrooms, quartered

BISCUITS

2 cups self-rising flour

¼ teaspoon salt

4 tablespoons (½ stick) cold unsalted butter, cut into small cubes

¾ cup buttermilk

1 egg, beaten

1. Preheat the oven to 250 degrees

2. On the stovetop, heat the butter and the tablespoon of olive oil over medium high heat in a large flameproof Dutch oven with a tight-fitting lid (or any oven-safe pot with lid) and brown the pancetta. Transfer the pancetta to a small bowl.

3. Pat the beef dry with paper towels and toss the beef in the flour. In small batches, over medium-high heat, add the beef to the remaining fat in the Dutch oven and brown on all sides, 8 to 10 minutes, adding more oil between batches as needed. Do not overcrowd the pan or the beef will become soggy and not brown properly. Transfer the browned beef to a large plate and set aside.

4. Lower the heat to medium and sauté the onions until softened and just beginning to brown. Deglaze the pot with the Worcestershire sauce, using a wooden spoon to loosen the browned bits on the bottom of the pot. Return the reserved beef and any juices to the pot. Add the carrots and celery and stir to combine with the beef. Pour in the stout and stock, making sure that it covers the beef. Add the pancetta, bay leaves, rosemary, salt, and pepper and bring to a boil.

5. Cover the pot with the lid, place in the oven, and continue to cook the stew for 1 hour and 15 minutes, checking the stew periodically and adding water as necessary. Add the mushrooms, replace the lid, and cook the stew for another 45 minutes, or until the beef and vegetables are tender. Remove the bay leaves.

6. When the stew is nearly cooked, prepare the biscuits. Sift the flour and salt into a large bowl. Add the butter and use a fork or your fingers to combine the butter with the flour mixture until it is crumbly. Stir in the buttermilk until the dough comes together. Turn the dough out onto a floured surface and knead briefly. Pat the dough into ¾ inch thickness and cut out rounds with a 2-inch biscuit cutter or a drinking glass.

7. Remove the stew from the oven. Increase the oven temperature to 400 degrees. Arrange the biscuits on the surface of the stew and brush the tops of the biscuits with the egg. When the oven temperature has reached 400 degrees, return the stew to the oven and bake uncovered for 10 to 12 minutes, until the biscuits are nicely browned.

GINGER CAKE WITH SYLLABUB

Once invited to join a political delegation to "supply any ginger that may be lacking" (*The Selected Letters of Bertrand Russell*), Russell, like the fiery root, could be counted on to enliven any gathering, and quipped that what "hunger is in relation to food, zest is in relation to life" (*The Conquest of Happiness*). This simple combination of spicy ginger cake and frothy syllabub pays tribute to the classic English trifle.

SYLLABUB

PREPARATION: 1 hour, 15 minutes (15 minutes active)

¼ cup sugar

2 teaspoons sherry (not cooking sherry)

1 teaspoon brandy

1 cup heavy cream

1. Combine the sugar, sherry, and brandy in a medium mixing bowl and stir until the sugar is dissolved.

2. Slowly add the cream to the sugar mixture and beat for about 5 minutes, or until soft peaks form.

3. Refrigerate for 1 hour before serving.

GINGER CAKE

PREPARATION: 1 hour, 30 minutes (15 minutes active)

½ cup (1 stick) plus 1 tablespoon unsalted butter

¾ cup dark corn syrup

1 cup packed light brown sugar

2 large eggs, lightly beaten

¼ cup heavy cream

2 cups all-purpose flour, plus more for flouring the pan

1 tablespoon ground ginger

½ teaspoon baking soda

½ teaspoon salt

1. Preheat the oven to 325 degrees. With 1 tablespoon butter, generously grease an 8 x 8-inch square pan and flour it.

2. In a medium saucepan over medium heat, melt the remaining ½ cup butter, add the corn syrup and brown sugar, stirring until smooth. Remove from the heat and let cool 10 to 15 minutes. Whisk in the eggs and cream.

3. In a large bowl, whisk together the flour, ginger, baking soda, and salt. Pour the butter mixture into the flour mixture and stir to combine.

4. Pour the batter into the prepared baking pan and bake for 40 to 45 minutes, until a knife blade inserted in the center of the cake comes out clean. Let cool in the pan for 5 minutes, then invert the cake onto a plate. Cut into squares of desired size and serve warm with a dollop of syllabub.

ENGLAND TO GO

Treat yourself to any film featuring Laurence Olivier, Emma Thompson, Judi Dench, or Trevor Howard. . . . See the Cliffs of Dover, Isle of Wight, Stratford-Upon-Avon, Stonehenge, and Leicester Square. . . . Tune into different eras by listening to composers Henry Purcell and Thomas Adès, meeting with authors/sisters Charlotte, Emily, and Anne Brontë, and letting director Alfred Hitchcock scare you. . . . Check out chef *Jamie's* (Oliver) *Food Revolution* and *Great Britain*, decide between the Wife of Bath and the Clerk in Chaucer's *The Canterbury Tales*, and pray for the Archbishop of Canterbury Thomas Becket. . . . Enjoy a tennis match played on the grass of Centre Court at the Wimbledon Championships, toasting Fred Perry and incredibly versatile fifteen-year-old champ Lottie Dod, learn about retired rugby star Ben Cohen's activism, and watch a replay of 2012 Olympic Gold Medal performances by runners Jessica Ennis and Mo Farah. . . . Bow to cinematic royalty: Helen Mirren starring in Stephen Frears's *The Queen*, Colin Firth in Tom Hooper's *The King's Speech*, and Charlie Chaplin in his *City Lights* and *Modern Times*. . . .

RESOURCES

PHILOSOPHY

The Basic Writings of Bertrand Russell by Bertrand Russell, edited by Robert E. Egner and Lester E. Denonn.

The Problems of Philosophy by Bertrand Russell: "The Value of Philosophy."

A History of Western Philosophy by Bertrand Russell.

MUSIC

Liege & Lief by Fairport Convention: "Come All Ye," "Farewell, Farewell."

Unplugged by Eric Clapton: "Layla," "Alberta," "Hey Hey."

A Modern Art by Claire Martin: "lowercase," "Nirvana," "So Twentieth Century."

Let It Be by the Beatles: "Across the Universe."

Revolver by the Beatles: "Tomorrow Never Knows."

Collection by Cleo Laine and Johnny Dankworth: "Stormy Weather," "If Music Be the Food of Love."

Time Remembered: John McLaughlin Plays Bill Evans by John McLaughlin.

Ocean's Kingdom by Paul McCartney, The London Classical Orchestra, John Wilson, conducting: "Ocean's Kingdom," "Moonrise."

The Best of Elvis Costello: The First 10 Years: "(What's So Funny 'bout) Peace, Love, and Understanding."

Interpretations: The British Rock Songbook by Bettye LaVette: "Love Reign O'er Me."

Quadrophenia by the Who: "Love Reign O'er Me."

FOOD

Food & Drink in Britain: From the Stone Age to the 19th Century by C. Anne Wilson.

"The Roast Beef of Old England" by Henry Fielding.

The Selected Letters of Bertrand Russell, Vol. 2: The Public Years, 1914–1970 by Bertrand Russell, edited by Nicholas Griffin.

The Conquest of Happiness by Bertrand Russell.

Persistence and Grace

MARCH IN BURMA

"Marietta, can you come out and play?" I answer with a bolt out the door when Sycamore and Josie, twelve- and nine-year-old neighbors, come calling. Throwbacks to simpler times, these kids find enchantment in the weather, any animal, dandelion salad, rope skipping and ball throwing, a toasty fireplace and hot chocolate. How did this happen? Their mother's gritty persistence has not been lost on them. Carrie, a single mother working a sixty-hour plus week at two restaurants, bolsters her wildly fluctuating income by giving sewing lessons and massages in her spare time. She laughs, recalling her most trying job, a four-month stint of eight-hour days spent removing staples from medical records in preparation for scanning. "You do what you have to do." She scrapes by financially, persevering hour by hour, coping with a car transmission beyond fixing and a landlord who ignores all repairs. Still, the cozy home shared by this trio exudes contentment.

Often I ask child philosophers: "What one idea, if you could understand it more clearly, would most benefit your life? What source of confusion trips you up repeatedly?" In all the years of asking this question, I've heard only once this surefire response from a child, her hand pledged over her name tag. "I want to know grace." This poised sixth grader was convinced that a firm grip on this concept would help her with sports, chores, friendships, everything—most especially, troubles. "I want to handle myself gracefully, or let grace handle me." She smiled as she uncovered her name tag. A girl unaware that she was already living up to her namesake, young Grace was on her way.

Carrie and her kids combine persistence and grace, doing what needs doing with quiet dignity, floating above difficulty by dealing with it straight on. They roll together through rocky monetary times and the children shift seamlessly from their mom's house to their dad's—some nights a feast of shrimp dumplings or roast chicken, and other evenings warmed plates of bean burritos or eggs and toast. As I watch Carrie the restaurant server squeeze through tiny spaces and deliver plates with delicacy that defuses patrons' impatience, I witness

grace in action. On her break from a twelve-hour day, she scurries to the sidelines of Sycamore's soccer game, cheering without an apparent care—on other days, she surprises Josie on her field trip. Talking Sycamore through the first angry throes of adolescent tempests and watching over Josie's underlying medical condition, Carrie manufactures grace from trouble. Striving for "unmuddled" lives for her children, she cheers on athlete Sycamore and participates with seamstress Josie. Carrie's grace seeps into her children's carriage. "Mom never gives up, stays positive even if she's worried, loves to laugh, and isn't afraid to say she's crazy about dessert" (all true for the kids, too). The sibling pals cherish their personal freedom, but assure me that rudeness and complaining aren't included in that freedom, ever.

Inquisitive minds of children, college students, back porch thinkers, and dinner companions want to know: How can I live, swarmed by difficulty and amidst disagreements, and persevere with some measure of ease? Can I win a peaceful mind and heart though life is tough? Given the glitches embedded in human nature, how can I rise above my antagonism and defensive boxing stance when problems arise?

Almost always these questions automatically shift the dialogue to a specific category of problems, talkative philosophers wagging an ashamed finger at the magnitude of difficulties we create for ourselves and for one another. Human-made adversity feels harder to handle because it isn't necessary. What causes us to multiply our problems? The number one answer popping up at philosophical gatherings: the pull of anger. We get mad at a world that guarantees misfortune, believing that we deserve easier and better circumstances. Habit-forming resentment foments. While the effects and prevalence of physical violence surround us, nonphysical cruelty mars our lives in a sinister fashion.

I join diners as we peer beneath the surface of ordinary-appearing affairs to spot undercurrents of hostility. We could talk until sunrise, despite the topic's unpleasantness, because the comprehension of this basic truth spurs us forward: We can't go after real problems until we stop going after one another. Around just one table we go. Brent's reenactment of his long-ago first (and last) day of law school is hilarious now, but the experience devastated him then. The professor strode to the podium, called on him randomly, and demanded that he stand. She asked that he define an abstruse legal term, *ad seriatim*, then another, *aliquot*. When he couldn't possibly answer, she haughtily announced that Brent would be the class dictionary for the rest of the semester. His sad skit over, Brent asks me to tell the group about my "twenty-four-hour rule," put into practice oh so fast in my teaching career. Gladly, I relate my oft-tested policy. I always hand students' papers back to them at the very end of the class period, and remind them (several times) that they must wait round the clock before venturing to my office to talk about their grades. One sterling example, in particular, of the rule's usefulness usually leaps to mind: "Yesterday I realized that your policy was meant for me . . . and lucky for you," a now-calm student once confessed. "When you wouldn't talk to me immediately, I lost it. I made an appointment with the dean to get a refund for the class. And I said some bad things about you in the student lounge. But my paper stunk."

Several voices now chime in with examples of hierarchical humiliation, those on top having their way with the administrative assistant and newest hire in the department. Next, an accountant's aide describes lingering chagrin at her employer's unveiled threats should she make known her findings of dodgy, client-pleasing bottom lines. Hesitant and then more confident diners bare their recent wounds inflicted by childhood bullies who never grew up: the boss berating a shy staff member, senior faculty members ostracizing the lone dissenting voice, neighbors shunning the gay couple on moving day. Language shows its fangs, whether careless or intentional. We trade examples of linguistic brush-offs: "No biggie," but it is huge to the worried person. "It's neither here nor there," but it is here and now for the one concerned. "It's all good," blithely ignores another's desperate cry that it's all bad.

Will we recognize the stupidity of beating our fists against the world? Can we learn to smooth out our relationships and quit seeking the upper hand? Is it possible for us to live together despite differences? Dare we hope for amicable disagreement?

Aung San Suu Kyi (AHNG-SAHN-SOO-CHEE), a nonviolent freedom fighter walking calmly through a barricade of loaded rifles in Burma, answers affirmatively to all the above. We've got the muster to seize trouble with style. Arriving for dinner with flowers in her hair, Aung San Suu Kyi toughens our resolve by massaging knotty, tensed hearts. Let's hear out this unassuming model of compelling persistence and unflappable grace.

PREPPING FOR BURMA

Read, watch, or listen to Aung San Suu Kyi's Nobel Lecture delivered in Oslo, Norway, on June 16, 2012. . . . Steamboat down the Irrawaddy River: discovering rice fields and mangroves in the Delta, shopping at bustling open-air markets in Mandalay, slowing down for a walk through the ancient city of Bagan, and beholding the Dhammayangyi Temple. . . . Learn about the ecological/human threat posed by the Dawei Development Project, follow the progressive Mizzima News started by Burmese exiles, and seek updates from the National League for Democracy. . . . Uncover the story behind "Unplayed Piano" sung by Irish songwriter Damien Rice and Lisa Hannigan, watch the Saffron Revolution unfold through the lens of valiant rebel reporters' handheld cameras in Anders Østergaard's documentary *Burma VJ*, and meet exiled monk Ashin Issariya (aka "King Zero"), one of the red-robed leaders of this 2007 massive protest and a founder of the All Burma Monks' Alliance. . . . Spend colonial British *Burmese Days* with novelist George Orwell and trace the history of the name change from Burma to Myanmar (me-ANN-MAR). . . .

I FELT THAT BEING UNDER HOUSE ARREST WAS PART OF MY JOB—I WAS DOING MY WORK.

AUNG SAN SUU KYI,
The Voice of Hope

Returning home to care for her ailing mother, Suu Kyi witnessed firsthand the brutal military dictatorship targeting both body and soul of the Burmese populace.

Equipped with an Oxford degree in politics, philosophy, and economics, plus her legacy as General Aung San's daughter, she never looked back at her comfortable life in England when her people looked to her to lead the nonviolent campaign for democratic reform. Armed with a tender heart and steely will, she endured almost two decades of harsh house arrest, stints in Insein prison, and ruptured family ties. She refused release from house arrest if it meant leaving Burma, dedicating her life to an overwhelming responsibility. "The Lady" was awarded the 1991 Nobel Peace Prize, and her peaceful, steadily successful fight now reverberates worldwide. While very few carry a load like hers, Suu Kyi's approach to difficulty assists anyone seeking endurance combined with inner elegance.

HARD

Let's fuel ourselves with her wisdom and dignity. How we approach the world makes all the difference. Soft entry into each day, flowing in our interactions with one another, activates our best qualities. In contrast, hard-hitting the new day with backbones rigid and ready for a fight blackens every attacker's eye. Suu Kyi recognized the danger of the following three A's, which none of us wants on our report cards. Anger, animosity, and aggression stand in the way of her work, just as they block ours.

Anger. . . . Suu Kyi readily admits that "I have a terrible temper" and "did bang the keys of the piano" (*Voice*) at times while under house arrest. Don't we all bang the keys? Diners offer ready examples of angry surges: yanking the sniffing dog's collar, thrusting with the big bang an unattended grocery cart, pacing with grinding teeth before the slow elevator, pounding the steering wheel impatiently, cursing the missed putt. "Where's my briefcase?!" Do we rage on, spewing and stewing? Or shall we agree with Suu Kyi that "melodrama is very silly. One has to live life on an even keel" (*Voice*)?

Head-shaking thinkers concur with their Burmese guide. Each of us bears the responsibility for diffusing anger's power by snatching it, tussling with it a bit, gaining the upper hand, and letting it go. Suu Kyi opted for daily meditation to quell her temper, her balanced perspective restored through quiet repose, and therefore she was "much less inclined to do things carelessly and unconsciously" (*Voice*). Knowing this unwelcome visitor packs a wallop, philosophers vow to best anger. End the upsetting phone call thoughtfully. Remove those aggravating tea bags left (daily!) in the sink.

Animosity. . . . Unchecked anger uncoils into animosity. Hatred overtakes the exhausted hater's life, proving ruinous from the inside out. "If I had really started hating my captors . . . the army, I would have defeated myself" (*Voice*). Suu Kyi finds hostility boring and debilitating, a tragic detour from the central task of improving oneself and the world. A child philosopher's riff on an old expression shows good grasp of ha-tred's self-inflicted damage: "I put myself into my own misery." Diners express the frenetic, obsessive quality of hatred. "I can't let it go." "It eats at me when I wake up." Anger may be impersonal, aimed at a flat tire, whereas animosity targets one or all. Suu Kyi repeats, encouragingly, that if we work diligently on controlling the mind, then reason can triumph over animosity by making us acutely aware of its stupidity. I picture my Burmese student Gum San's startled reaction to the hatred directed by classmates at a politician for that now elected official's stance, at a celebrity for alleged misconduct, at a former friend for leaving town. Gentle Gum San's admiration for Suu Kyi's philosophy was my first introduction to her. He did her proud in class by articulating his lack of hatred for the dictatorship that he fled, focusing instead on maximizing his new freedom.

Aggression. . . . Animosity, fanned over time, unravels into aggression. I queasily recall my discomfort as one of five panel participants debating the pros and cons of the U.S. invasion of Iraq. Casting a furious glare in my direction upon arrival, a man took his seat in the second row. His belligerence escalated with his every interruption of my remarks, all of which I delivered in question form. His swollen fury now conspicuous to all in attendance, he started toward me, lurching over the front row seats.

Rumble alert?

Dinner partners share less obvious but no less alarming sorry tales of aggression. Insults, teasing, mocking, and taunting all strike fear, the recipient worried what's next. Child and college philosophers speak up about venom unleashed from the solitary computer screen, calling it "cowardly," "never anonymous," "your total responsibility." Misdirected nastiness drops with a thud into a recipient's inbox, the sender's aggression satisfied, the fallout beginning.

Diners push chairs back from the table, fed up with this tough stuff, ready for a spongy diet.

SOFT

The three A's now outed, persisting in this inner war, Suu Kyi's words ring true: "I don't give up trying to be a better person . . . a battle that will go on my whole life" (*Voice*). Gradually we soften and strengthen, becoming more gelatin than cinderblock.

We wade into turbulent waters and swim, reinforced by qualities Suu Kyi brings to bear in her work toward a democratic Burma. Imagine a day armed with Suu Kyi's trusty weapons of humor, compromise, and kindness—these top three adopted repeatedly by philosophers of all stripes. A daily dose of such softeners increases by leaping bounds the steady presence of persistence and grace.

How hard to live without a sense of humor. Suu Kyi frequently extols its lifelong benefits. Wittiness lends objectivity as it gives the laugher a step outside the problem and welcome moments of distance and reprieve. Serving as a mental health tonic, humor helps her see "the ridiculous side of things . . . seeing the absurd and funny side . . . and you don't take your troubles so seriously anymore" (*Voice*). Armed guards on patrol to prevent the escape of a frail woman with no desire to leave Burma? Ha! She longed for a friendly Saturday tea and conversation with leading military officials. To the suggestion that they would surely refuse the invitation, her response draws dinner table laughs: "We could always have coffee" ("The First Lady of Freedom," *Time*, January 10, 2011). Hear! Hear! Voices attest to laughter's power. Children claim it "unleashes me," and "stops my craziness." Humor dulls grief's ache. Lee, coping secretly with a terminal illness, leads our class in his everyday practice of "laughing meditation," our group hilarity drawing curious onlookers into laughter's stress-releasing clarity. Laughter delivers a fresh perspective.

How hard to live without compromise. Burma's "Lady" opens negotiations with trust and without deceit, prepared to work for the best possible outcome. Immaturely clinging to one ironclad policy accomplishes nothing because "in politics one has to be flexible" (*Voice*). When she demonstrates commitment to compromise, tension loosens and impasses melt. Suu Kyi searches for points of agreement, repeatedly proves her willingness to listen, readily asks for help. She masters "the technique of getting to know people: tell us what you have to say," she invites (*Voice*). If she or her colleagues make mistakes, she hastens an apology.

Diners reflect before speaking. An embattled corporate executive shares his response to insulting remarks: "What do you think I did? Tell me what you've heard." Off guard but no longer on guard, his protagonist chats in lowered voice. Philosophers acknowledge their previous use of intimidation and suffer now-productive embarrassment: A coach pushes her players too far, berating their inadequacy in too-intense drills; parents coerce children into achieving ever-higher grades, ignoring their requests for downtime; one spouse ups the pressure on the other to attain career advancement—or else. Using the wrong way to get their way, relationships harden—ballplayers skip practice, children close books, the partnership dissolves. Problems rather than people persist. In contrast, the give and take of compromise stretches the realm of what's possible. "You can always find a way" (*Voice*) and newly informed philosophers resolve to find sensible, more dignified ways to coach, to parent, and to love, keeping options and ears open.

How hard to live without giving and receiving kindness, acting "to respond with sensitivity and human warmth to the hopes and needs of others" ("Nobel Lecture," June 16, 2012). Suu Kyi's gratitude that "in my life, I have been showered with kindness" (*Time*) explains her desire to return this biggest favor of all, to all. Her practice of kindness saw her through danger and despair, as her yielding yet rugged way wore down obstacles. Suu Kyi won election to parliament, proudly representing the township of Kawhmu and offering hope for democratic reforms. She travels abroad and speaks to huge crowds of international supporters. This humble world leader insists that kindness can change any life it touches. I bring her these further testimonies to the clout of kindness. Gentle approaches rise above hard times in these glimpses of persistence and grace.

Determined to honor the brother he lost on 9/11, Don and his wife unite with other victims' families in assuring nonviolent and productive responses to that day. Their ongoing efforts support women and children in Afghanistan, focusing on education and job training for Afghan widows. "Broadness of vision" (*Voice*) guides the members of this group who, like Suu Kyi, are too busy for thoughts of vengeance. In a hardscrabble town with houses and hopes rapidly foreclosing, an intervention specialist starts an elementary school philosophy club. Meditation calms the children's anxiety, and one lonely, tough-luck child grows more into herself with each discussion. Soon, KaeLah shows kindness to the school bully, befriending the outcast and raising money on the sly for his destitute family. KaeLah's teacher delivers a holiday feast, blankets and coats for all, plus electronic equipment that the anonymous donor did not possess. Four more snapshots of triumphant kindness: A young mother, sitting between quarreling brothers, flips through their scrapbook filled with happy times, the conflict soon over. Ann and Robert care for her two completely dependent siblings for more than fifty years, persisting through chronic medical issues and bureaucratic snafus without a blink and with contagious compassion. A physical therapist demonstrates to frustrated staff members the art of touch—Julie places her hand just so and the patient relaxes, now turning and moving with the soft feel of her warm hand. Nurse Wanda twirls on clicking heels while reaching here and there, smoothing foreheads, telling tales, relieving apprehension, then heads home to tend to her dying mother.

How often has kindness lightened your step and enabled your perseverance? Count and count the ways. "More than love, I value kindness . . . kindness remains" (*Time*). One diner spoke for many: "Far from cliché, kindness makes it all worth it."

Kindness doubles as a master key, unlocking doors with its greasing properties: persistence and grace.

~~~~~~~~~~~~~~~~~~~~~~~~~~~~

AND YOUR TOPIC FOR DINNER CONVERSATION IS

It was a photograph splashed across front pages round the world. Aung San Suu Kyi, standing tall behind bars, greeted thousands of supporters on the day of her release from house arrest. As outstretched hands reached toward her, she smiled and spoke with clear affection: "We haven't seen each other for so long. I have so much to tell you" ("Myanmar Junta Frees Dissident; Crowds Gather," *The New York Times*, November 14, 2010). What has Suu Kyi told *you*? What lesson stands out? Be specific about ways that you can incorporate her peaceful way with difficulty into your everyday life.

~~~~~~~~~~~~~~~~~~~~~~

THE DOORBELL RINGS

Encourage guests' imaginations in choosing tea, beer, a tart white wine, or any beverage that complements Burmese food's spiciness. Defying the military by carrying their black lacquerware alms bowls upside down during the Saffron Revolution, Burmese monks poignantly transformed their everyday dishes into symbols of peaceful persistence. Pay tribute to their dogged grace by serving the evening's meal using brightly colored red or orange bowls and trays that recall the protesting monks' saffron-hued robes. In Burmese homes, food is served family-style on large, table-sized platters. These lacquerware platters (*byat*) are modern versions of the refined trays that were used by Burmese royalty. For dessert anticipate your host's surprise, the dessert he or she would miss the most if restricted for so many years, as was Suu Kyi.

U Yee Nwe's *Spellbinding Piano of Burma* transports you to his homeland. Sample the culture with his "Phone Moe Thun Long" ("The Power Rains Down Upon the Kingdom") and "Sandaya Let Swan Pya" ("Piano Improvisations on a Medley"). Bach and Mozart were Suu Kyi's constant companions during her periods of forced confinement, Bach providing calm and Mozart joy. Enjoy the light touch of the Modern Jazz Quartet's *Blues on Bach*, the foursome's blues originals interspersed with their interpretations of Bach classics. Bask in the sounds of the Quartet's "Precious Joy," "Tears from the Children," and "Rise Up in the Morning." Let the meshing of Hilary Hahn's violin with Natalie Zhu's piano flood the room with Mozart's unmistakable sound. Try selections from three of his Sonatas for Piano and Violin: in F, the Allegro and Rondo; in G, the Allegro; and in E Minor, Tempo di minuetto. Settle in for tonight's discussion, supported by music that Suu Kyi loves.

Glenn Gould plays Bach's *The Well-Tempered Clavier* like no other. Use the number of each person's birthday as a way of choosing among the forty-eight varieties of prelude and fugue. Gould's piano gracefully moves with Bach through each of the major and minor keys and adds another voice to your conversation. Lean back in comfort with pianist Alfred Brendel's playing of Bach's Chromatic Fantasia and Fugue in D Minor. Lean into the heart of your talk buoyed by the Bach Chaconne, delivered memorably by Hilary Hahn's bow and strings. Stop and listen for a few minutes,

Hahn's love for this piece is contagious. As you wrap up your dialogue, Mozart rouses you with his invitation to "The Hunt." Kick back to the four movements of this String Quartet No. 17 in B-flat.

The pace quickens with the guitar-backed vocals of Lay Phyu's soft rock. Taste a little Burmese nightlife with his "Ale Akoi," "Than Yaw Zin," "Dali Nih," and "Aluaan." Suu Kyi has a loyal fan in Bono, lead singer of the Irish band U2. His stirring plea for an end to her imprisonment rang out worldwide in 2001, Bono encouraging her to "Walk On" and singing convincingly that "what you got / they can't steal it," though the dictatorship could and did ban the recording. Celebrate her release with U2's "Beautiful Day" and "Grace." As is the custom in Burmese homes at evening's end, sip black tea sweetened with condensed milk. As you part company, stride into the night, primed for tomorrow by U2's prayer for "Peace on Earth."

In the Kitchen

GRATED MANGO SALAD

Buddhist monks meditated among mango groves thousands of years ago, their purposeful daily routines keeping pace with the slow ripening of the fleshy mango. The pervasive flavor of this sweetly-sour fruit anchors Burmese cuisine, reminding diners of sacred Buddhist texts featuring the ancient stone fruit. Although mangoes originated in India, traveling Buddhists brought them to Burma, where they became staple ingredients in spicy salads. In this version, salty fish sauce meshes with brown sugar and tart lime for a classically Burmese combination of tastes.

PREPARATION: 30 minutes

2 tablespoons fish sauce

2 tablespoons packed brown sugar

3 tablespoons fresh lime juice

½ teaspoon dried red pepper flakes

3 firm mangoes

2 cups bean sprouts

½ cup chopped scallions

¼ cup chopped fresh mint

½ cup chopped fresh cilantro

½ cup coarsely chopped roasted cashews

1. Mix together the fish sauce, brown sugar, lime juice, and pepper flakes. Set aside this dressing.

2. Peel the mangoes. Using a small, sharp knife, slice the fruit into thin spears. (If you prefer, and your mangoes are very firm, grate the flesh of the mangoes using the largest holes of a box grater, taking care to avoid the large pits.)

3. Combine the mangoes, sprouts, scallions, mint, and cilantro in a serving bowl. Drizzle with the dressing and toss to coat. Sprinkle the cashews on top.

TOFU CURRY

With its sharp-tasting curries made from blends of spices and herbs—usually onion, garlic, ginger, and turmeric—Burmese food reveals complex flavors one slow bite at a time. Rhythmically pounded into curry pastes or crushed into powders for dyeing the saffron-colored robes of Buddhist monks, turmeric—with its distinctive shade of orange—holds a permanent place of honor in monasteries and homes, where curry might be consumed several times a day.

PREPARATION: 1 hour, 30 minutes

2 pounds firm tofu, each block cut into two halves lengthwise and gently pressed between paper towels to remove excess water

3 onions, 2 chopped, 1 thinly sliced

6 cloves garlic, peeled and minced

1-inch piece of fresh ginger, peeled and cut into small chunks

1 teaspoon ground turmeric

½ teaspoon dried red pepper flakes

1 teaspoon salt

¼ cup sesame oil

6–7 large plum tomatoes, seeded and diced (approximately 4 cups)

½ cup water

2 tablespoons fish sauce

2-inch piece of lemon grass, thinly sliced

2 limes, juiced

2 serrano or other minced chiles, or to taste

1 pound cellophane noodles

½ cup chopped fresh cilantro

1. Cut the tofu into 1-inch cubes and set aside.

2. Using a food processor (or a mortar and pestle), combine the chopped onions, garlic, ginger, turmeric, pepper flakes, and salt and process or mash into a thick paste.

3. Heat a wok or large sauté pan with high sides over medium-high heat. Add the sesame oil and heat until a droplet or two of water evaporates upon contact.

4. Add the paste and cook over medium heat for 4 to 5 minutes. Add the tofu and sliced onion and toss with the paste until well coated, 1 to 2 minutes. Add the tomatoes and ½ cup water and cook for 3 to 4 minutes, then add the fish sauce, lemon grass, lime juice, and chiles. Cover and cook for 2 to 3 minutes, then uncover and continue to cook for 5 to 10 minutes, or until the liquid has slightly reduced.

5. Meanwhile, prepare the cellophane noodles according to the package instructions.

6. Remove the curry from the heat and stir in the cilantro. Serve in noodle-filled bowls.

BURMA TO GO

Hike the caves and gorges in Shan State, followed by a boating excursion through the floating vegetable gardens of Inle Lake with your "leg rower" Intha guide. . . . Read Peter Popham's *The Lady and the Peacock*, Thant Myint U's *The River of Lost Footsteps: A Personal History of Burma*, and Zoya Phan's *Undaunted: My Struggle for Freedom and Survival in Burma*. . . . Watch Luc Besson's *The Lady*, starring Michelle Yeoh as Suu Kyi, pour over news clips of the 8888 Uprising for democracy highlighted by Suu Kyi's first major speech to more than 500,000 protesters at the Shwedagon Pagoda, and then see this story retold and time period relived in *Beyond Rangoon*, directed by John Boorman and starring U Aung Ko. . . . Move your feet and knees in the dancing sport of *chinlone*, juggling the rattan ball while kicking up your heels in a circle of teammates. . . .

Splash in the New Year come mid-April during the Water Festival, listening for sounds of bamboo clappers, gongs, and xylophones. . . . Appreciate the artistry of Aung Win on piano and female hip-hop artist Sandi Myint Lwin on stage. . . .

RESOURCES

PHILOSOPHY

The Voice of Hope: Conversations with Alan Clements by Aung San Suu Kyi.

"The First Lady of Freedom" by Hannah Beech, *Time*, January 10, 2011.

"Nobel Lecture" by Aung San Suu Kyi, delivered in Oslo, Norway, June 16, 2012.

"Myanmar Junta Frees Dissident; Crowds Gather," *The New York Times*, November 14, 2010.

MUSIC

Spellbinding Piano of Burma by U Yee Nwe: "Phone Moe Thun Long" ("The Power Rains Down Upon the Kingdom"), "Sandaya Let Swan Pya" ("Piano Improvisations on a Medley").

Blues on Bach by Modern Jazz Quartet: "Precious Joy," "Tears from the Children," "Rise Up in the Morning."

Mozart Violin Sonatas K. 301, 304, 376, & 526 by Wolfgang Amadeus Mozart, Hilary Hahn, violin, and Natalie Zhu, piano: Sonata for Piano and Violin in F, K. 376: Allegro, Rondo; Sonata for Piano and Violin in G, K. 301: Allegro; Sonata for Piano and Violin in E Minor, K. 304: Tempo di minuetto.

The Glenn Gould Edition—Bach: The Well-Tempered Clavier, Book I by Johann Sebastian Bach, Glenn Gould, piano.

The Glenn Gould Edition—Bach: The Well-Tempered Clavier, Book II by Johann Sebastian Bach, Glenn Gould, piano.

Bach: Italian Concerto BMV 971; Chromatic Fantasia and Fugue BMV 903 by Johann Sebastian Bach, Alfred Brendel, piano: Chromatic Fantasia and Fugue in D Minor, BMV 903.

Bach: Partitas for Solo Violin by Johann Sebastian Bach, Hilary Hahn, violin: Partita no. 2 for Violin in D Minor, BMV 1004: Chaconne.

Mozart: The String Quartets by Wolfgang Amadeus Mozart, Amadeus Quartet, performing: String Quartet no. 17 in B-flat, K. 458: "The Hunt."

Bay of Bangle by Lay Phyu: "Ale Akoi," "Than Yaw Zin," "Dall Nlh," "Aluaan."

All That You Can't Leave Behind by U2: "Walk On," "Beautiful Day," "Grace," "Peace on Earth."

FOOD

A History of Food by Maguelonne Toussaint-Samat.

Community and the Melting Pot

APRIL IN CHICAGO

Students in my ethics class welcomed April's signs of new life. Beginning in January, individuals from the widest variety of backgrounds bravely investigated the roots of large social problems and the wrenching manifestation of those issues in their personal lives. Hunger, poverty, environmental disaster, violence, ethnic and gender bias, access to health and child care, end of life decisions—all tackled honestly and respectfully. Together we struggled for possible solutions to problems that were better grasped as students volunteered their own painful experiences—a grand-father's refusal of life-prolonging treatment, the effects of exposure to asbestos, and the struggle to break free from a destructive past.

Laughing in our familiar circle for our last class meeting, the hum of animated conversations stopped suddenly and I heard the words that guarantee teacher surprise: "Go on and tell her," a classmate urged his grinning accomplice. What could they tell me at this late date? "We've decided that we want to marry you and also marry each other. Go with us to city hall to apply for a license legitimizing our 'civil union.' You know we meet the requirements. Let's challenge the system!" What fun we had talking (and *only* talking) about their "proposal."

Philosophy circles naturally create a sense of belonging. Community happens when people link minds and hearts in a shared desire to understand the world better and to live more fully. Heartfelt exchanges allow people to know one another and trust builds in a communal atmosphere. I watch as individuals thrive on connection—names memorized and eye contact secured, they sit more confidently and more at ease. Ian writes persuasively on his final exam about his experience in my almost-married ethics class: "Free flowing ideas and language were the tools of success. There was no winner or loser, there was only understanding, not only of the issue but of the people themselves. No angry shouting matches or silly rhetoric. Instead compromise and collaboration won the day. This course set the stage for amicable teamwork and meaningful human interaction. A community was born

of people from urban and rural areas of Virginia, Bangladesh, Thailand, Germany, Nigeria, Brazil, and Argentina."

Discussion of universal themes unites participants in all sorts of settings. Diners report anticipation as the big evening draws near, notepads filling up, chats and e-mails increasing between meetings. Every time I talk with new friends around a philosophy table, I catch the consistent happiness found in camaraderie. Linda's unmasked joy at the end of a teacher workshop that focused on sharing philosophy with children evoked a cheer: "We got to *talk* to each other about our educational ideals, personal lives, our backgrounds. We never do *that*. It was like a holiday. We're organizing summer outings." After a year of bimonthly meetings, a philosophy club of heretofore strangers made plans for year two. "Each of us can invite someone new to join us. And we may hook up in smaller groups between sessions." Middle school philosophers begged their club adviser for all-day Saturday meetings. (Yes, it's true.) "We need more time to hang out. An hour after school isn't enough. Please? If we serve lunch maybe even more teachers will come."

Feeling alone in a world full of people comes with the human condition. That unsettling tug of something akin to exile is as old as we are. It creeps up on us jammed shoulder-to-shoulder in a subway, squeezed into a spot for the photograph at family reunions, laughing during our own birthday parties. Now, a new and often underrated source of separation accompanies the recent and still-unfolding revolution in technology. For all of the benefits derived from computer and Internet, cell phone and satellite dish, the dramatic misuse of these tools results in severed connections in real life. I wish I had fewer examples from which to draw. In the actual presence of vacationing family and friends, heads bow to screens and fingers tap, most ironically, on "social networking sites." Headphones stay put during car rides and dinner. The superinten-

dent of schools looks out with a frozen stare from the graduation platform, his cloaked fingers sending text messages throughout the ceremony. While a nervous student reads original poetry aloud, her best friend sits in the front row, fidgeting with a "smart" phone camouflaged (not!) by her backpack. Students complain of anxiety attacks caused by my requirement that phones buzz off before class. But those same students lament their "terrible addiction to technology." Too late, their papers and talks after class reveal, they realize that they are no longer a part of their old social circle. Though fully wired, they dropped the lines of communication. Relationships fray, and virtual reality proves no substitute for face-to-face authenticity.

We wrestle with the hunger for community in an often splintered world that can make belonging seem out of reach. Though the rift of separation and need to mend it may not be fully conscious, the pleasures of community wash over us. Rather than homogenizing individuals, communal groups naturally absorb differences. Privacy is invaluable, but without community we wander the planet unmoored. Active belonging complements the respite of solitude.

Not long ago, I was asked at a book talk for one solid reason to have faith in the future of the planet. Next question, please! My unrehearsed response flowed immediately and with unexpected emotion: "Witnessing over and over the healing power found within inclusive community provides the surest source of hope for me. The human capacity for empathy, the willingness to be with those in pain and to stay there, to exult in others' successes and to join in the celebration, makes a believer out of me. People in your town and in mine, in Egypt and Alabama, in Afghanistan and Japan, in Missouri and Haiti, surround those who are physically and emotionally wounded and hold on tight. Connections seal and multiply." Audience members jumped in with further examples: Cancer survivors finding strength and purpose in numbers, moving in step in exercise class, and walking to raise money for the cure. Caregivers of Alzheimer's patients embracing at a hospital party and exchanging contact information. Residents of a small town swarming into the center square, welcoming home the young war veteran. A dozen grade school friends discovering middle age together as a team during their summer softball league. A bridge club spanning three generations. . . .

Scrubbing pans and passing platters, Jane Addams defined community for the melting pot that was Chicago at the collision of the nineteenth and twentieth centuries. Wanting "a free mind and unfettered kindliness" (*Peace and Bread in Time of War*) for all, she dished up true comfort food for the masses. What might this dishwasher and winner of the Nobel Peace Prize be cooking just for us?

PREPPING FOR CHICAGO

Listen! Rambunctious bluesman Lonnie Brooks welcomes you to his *Sweet Home Chicago*, Curtis Mayfield soulfully motions to "Move on Up" *and* "Get Down," Kurt Elling sings he's "Goin' to Chicago" live from the Green Mill Jazz Club, and Patricia Barber invites you in song to be her *Companion*. . . . Satisfied by a slice of deep-dish pizza, treat yourself at no charge to a classical concert in Grant Park's Pritzker Pavilion and to the five-day Chicago Dancing Festival spanning the Windy City in August. . . . Make merry with dinner and a show at The Second City, home of improv comedy that boasts of alumni Tina Fey and Stephen Colbert, Steve Carell and Gilda Radner. . . . Join Ira Glass, host of Chicago Public Radio's *This American Life*, in "Episode 84. Harold" and get to know Mayor Harold Washington, listen to a recording of any live interview conducted by maestro Studs Terkel on WFMT, and fast tap with the "Lord of the Dance," Michael Flatley. . . .

> CERTAIN SOCIAL SENTIMENTS . . . LIKE ALL HIGHER AIMS LIVE ONLY BY COMMUNION AND FELLOWSHIP, CULTIVATED MOST EASILY IN THE FOSTERING SOIL OF COMMUNITY LIFE.
>
> JANE ADDAMS,
> *Peace and Bread in Time of War*

Resident/manager of the first settlement house in Chicago, globetrotting pacifist, social reformer—imagining Jane Addams's daily routine leaves me breathless. She created community from chaos, honored the timeless link between food and peace, treated huge obstacles as everyday hurdles, all with steadfast grit. Thousands of lonely people caught whiffs of food wafting from Hull-House and followed the scent of homecoming. Her prayer continues at your table that "the great mother breasts of our common humanity . . . may never be withheld from you" (*Twenty Years at Hull-House*). A delegate to the 1912 Progressive Party convention, Addams lived her philosophy. Here's what happened.

ISOLATION

Everywhere I go I find ready agreement with Addams's conviction that "we are all more or less familiar with the results of isolation" (*Twenty Years*). Don't we all feel the stranger at times? When difference unsettles and insecurity smarts, invisible fences keep us out—ethnic and socioeconomic, age and gender, educational and occupational, dialect and physical appearance. Some describe the futile sensation of standing on the perimeter of already-formed groups. Others confess never having experienced the perks of communal life. Many

echo Ian's assessment: "Interaction should be achieved easily, but instantaneous communication has run amok and provided its own barriers, drowning out meaningful connections in a torrent of noise."

From her early years in Cedarville, Illinois, until her death, in 1935, Jane Addams experienced the world as an outsider. By her account, an "ugly, pigeon-toed little girl, whose crooked back obliged her to walk with her head held very much to one side" (*Twenty Years*), she walked a pace or two behind the father she adored so as not to embarrass him. Upon her graduation from Rockford Seminary in 1881, she sought to follow her father's lead into public service and soon discovered that the options for women to participate in public life were few. Bitten again by the sting of the misfit, she embarked upon the almost-obligatory trip to Europe expected for young women of her social class. No work of art or glimpse of finery touched her heart like the slums swelling with London's starving. One sight grabbed her conscience and never let go. "Nothing is so fraught with significance as the human hand, this oldest tool" (*Twenty Years*), and upward stretching hands begging for a scrap of food served as her life's motivation. Always able to identify with the outcast, she writes compellingly of the "forlorn feeling that occasionally seizes upon you when you arrive early in the morning a stranger in a great city" (*Twenty Years*). Chicago's metropolitan mix proved the perfect outlet for her passion to extend her own outstretched hand.

The industrial revolution shook the Western world, its machines uprooting agricultural, small-town life. At the turn of the twentieth century, millions of African-Americans left the familiarity of rural living and the bite of racism in the South, Midwest, and on the West Coast and, like the throngs of unemployed departing the European countryside, made haste for industrial centers and the promise of better lives. Sails set and feet fled, Chicago-bound. How could one city absorb this huge influx of newcomers who had no understanding of factory and tenement life and were often unable to speak English? How would laborers already in the clutches of bosses and sweatshops treat these new job seekers? Where to go to find a breath of fresh air, quiet, or any reminder of home? How to ask for a job, directions, or a hand up? At the mercy of weather extremes and rampant contagious illnesses, what to do? Addams knew. Give sanctuary to the desperate, a place to call their own. Feed and teach. Doors flung open to one and all in 1889, Hull-House, on Halsted Street, serving as refuge for the homeless and dispirited, beckoning some twenty nationalities inside.

Addams would continually "feel curiously outside" walking on her "own proper path" that required her "to leave the traditional highway" (*Peace and Bread*). She endured opposition to her settlement, to her pacifist stance before the outbreak of World War I, and to her campaigns for social justice. At Hull-House the rebel mandated civility, religious diversity, day care for kids, inclusion of the elderly, and cautioned the best athletes against the perils of professional sports. Oddball! Still, at the conclusion of her many trips, Addams came home to her community of thousands at Hull-House, her lingering sense of "aloneness" quenched by the "quick sense of human fellowship" (*Twenty Years*).

"The misfit made misfits fit!" a child philosopher clapped. How? Filling cups and peeling potatoes.

FUSION

Sifting bran through cupped hands and rubbing wheat between her fingers, this daughter, granddaughter, and great-granddaughter of millers grasped the unbreakable connection between food and peaceful living. Picture the young girl held aloft in big, dusty hands, her happiest childhood occupation spent gazing at the "foaming water wheel turning" (*Peace and Bread*) yellow wheat into white flour, the warmth of bread and milk soon to follow. How could she provide such comfort and security for those without?

Hitch up your skirt and roll up that pant leg! Today we accept Addams's invitation to spend the day at Hull-House. It's 1895 and we're late. Off we go:

Halsted Street runs for thirty-two miles and our walk thrusts us into a bustling center of industrial whistles, sharp cries of street vendors, and shift workers quickstepping from tenement to factory. We spot a "foothold of a house" sandwiched between an undertaker and a saloon on the West Side of Chicago. Sounds and smells compete: a chorus singing Handel's *Messiah*, the aroma of coffee mixing with the scent of hot dogs and sauerkraut, shouts of children at play, voices engaged in spirited debate, the clatter of overturned garbage cans, a scuffle between volunteers and cocaine dealers. A talkative group from the University of Chicago alights from a rickety carriage and trails a quartet of philanthropists in fancy dress into a true hospitality house.

We step inside. A master welder has fashioned community from a melting pot of humanity. Pots boil in a frenzied kitchen—volunteers wash breakfast dishes with lunch preparation in full swing. A child runs by and requests mac 'n' cheese fixed the way *he* likes it. Heads converge over a small stove for a spontaneous cooking lesson. Nimble hands knead dough, chop vegetables, and ladle steaming bowls of soup. As teachers conduct English classes, "foreign colonies which so easily isolate themselves" (*Twenty Years*) now sit together, twisting their tongues to shape new sounds. Women residents in the "Jane Club" celebrate their successful group protest for first-time safety measures at the garment factory while a packed room buzzes with talk of forming trade unions. Ignoring obvious differences, Irish-Catholic and Austrian-Jew unite over steeping cups of tea in their opposition to sweatshops and child labor. Collaboration colors all activities. Preparing for the evening's dance, organizers shoo reluctant players of all ages from the gymnasium. Drama, music, poetry, and philosophy clubs congregate. Incoming and outgoing letters and packages link lives at a post office branch. Chairs are rearranged in the drawing room for the weekly afternoon concert regularly enjoyed by the neighboring elderly—a buffet table of specialties from the "old countries" awaits at the entrance.

What a day. Does anyone ever take permanent leave of Hull-House, such vivid testimony to the "solidarity of the human race" (*Twenty Years*)? Think of the ever-outward spiraling effects of her work—for generations, some two thousand visitors a day found a home at *their* community center. I thought hard about her legacy when I visited faculty and students at Chicago's Truman College. A world map pinpointing students' homelands hangs at the entrance:

One hundred and sixty countries represented and ninety languages are spoken on the grounds of this community college! Often hailed as democracy's college, with its diversity of on-the-move students who juggle school and other commitments, the human mix at these fast-paced campuses mirrors our society, offering a good test case for Addams's way.

Yes, food cements connections especially well in this setting. I tasted it in Chicago as I do in Charlottesville, cooking, serving, and passing bread providing an "outlet for that sentiment of universal brotherhood" (*Twenty Years*). As students feel more a part of their philosophizing circle, they predictably ask if they "can bring food for the class." Over and over, food melts differences. A class big in number becomes intimate in size with the help of spring rolls and special sauce. A more delicate, earnest tone laces dialogue, as students who have shared the same room for months somehow "know" one another better. Shy students speak without hesitation—talkative, somewhat strong-willed philosophers listen instead. Food acts as philosophy's ally in countless settings. Squeezing limes and chopping vegetables, the owner of a stone and tile shop gathers architects and stonemasons, woodworkers and movie makers around an oak-hewn table for our once-a-month philosophizing. Canapés enhance conversation about flexibility at a Pilates studio. Muffins break the ice on Philosophy Friday at the senior center.

Without fail Addams and Hull-House bring dinner-table talk to a boil. Addams leaves nourishing leftovers with no expiration date. Sample just a taste of her influence—Addams making good on her insistence that food can build communities heightens our awareness. "I can't remember sitting down with others for a meal until our first gathering. I'm going to make it a practice in other places. The very act *does* give birth to community." Many new visitors to Hull-House are moved to take a close look at their immediate community *as* a community. "Where might a cooked meal go a long way? Rescue squads, refugee centers, emergency shelters for women and children, an afterschool program, elderly neighbors, working single parents, a sad home. . . ." Service and social life take on fresh importance. Group efforts hold more promise and diners make plans. Like a song performed by the Hull-House Music Club, a project "receives in exchange for the music of isolated voices the volume and strength of chorus" (*Twenty Years*).

Jane Addams never grows old. Now you know her secret.

───────────

AND YOUR TOPIC FOR DINNER CONVERSATION IS

"But more gratifying than any understanding or response from without could possibly be was the consciousness that a growing group of residents

was gathering at Hull-House, held together in that soundest of all social bonds, the companionship of mutual interests" (*Twenty Years*). Discuss the companionable community evolving from your gatherings round the Philosopher's Table. Take turns describing what belonging to this group adds to your life. What "mutual interests" do you share? Do you agree with Addams that "the social relation is essentially a reciprocal relation" (*Twenty Years*)? Explain.

───────────

THE DOORBELL RINGS

Guests embrace the spirit of American potluck gatherings by contributing a small side dish from their countries of origin. Showcasing the group's diversity, diners can supply a sampling of beer, wine, or any favorite beverage from the "homeland." Several guests should tuck a fresh baked loaf under an arm, certainly one of the hearty oatmeal varieties popular in Addams's day. Everyone pitch in to assemble the checkerboard cookies while snacking on Mini Chicago Dogs.

"Rumble Thy Bellyful" with fiddler Liz Carroll and her international gathering of String Sisters. Carroll and John Doyle pay fine tribute to Chicago's Irish music tradition, and their request for "A Pound a Week Rise" could be a Hull-House anthem. Muddy Waters lures you away from the duo's *Double Play*, bragging correctly, "I've Got My Mojo Working." Need this iconic representative of the Chicago Blues ask "Baby, Please Don't Go"? Traveling with his guitar and the acoustic blues tradition of the Mississippi Delta, Waters may well have trekked along the road that "winds from Chicago to L.A." Ride with Nat King Cole and "(Get Your Kicks on) Route 66," checking the sky as he croons "It's Only a Paper Moon." Jazz vibraphonist Jason Adasiewicz suggests that your group "Get in There," his

Sun Rooms providing a smooth segue into tonight's discussion.

A jazz concert was featured in Carnegie Hall for the first time in 1938 and the famed venue shook to "One O'Clock Jump," "Avalon," and "Sing Sing Sing." The clarinet-waving bandleader with eastern European roots got his start in the Hull-House Boys Club Band! "Some of the pupils in the music school have developed during the years into trained musicians and are supporting themselves in their chosen profession" (*Twenty Years*). Benny Goodman proved Addams right. Let his innovative style and integrated band inspire your conversation. Renowned musical collaborator Herbie Hancock, founder of The International Committee of Artists for Peace, assembles musicians around the world to participate in *The Imagine Project*. "Don't Give Up" as "A Change Is Gonna Come," voices chime encouragingly. *Blowing in from Chicago* on his saxophone, jazzman Clifford Jordan puts the finishing touches on your philosophizing.

Hull-House ledgers showed large weekly coffee orders, so sit in with the regulars for a piping hot cup. Belting out the "First Time I Met the Blues," guitarist Buddy Guy signals his departure with a shout to "Give Me My Coat and Shoes." Koko Taylor counters with a tease to "Let the Good Times Roll." Tarry to consider her offer that "You Can Have My Husband" and then "Wang Dang Doodle" into a happy night.

MINI CHICAGO DOGS

Filled with noisy bartering and chatter, the open-air Maxwell Street Market was a boisterous point of cultural exchange for the newest settlers of Addams's neighborhood. Hawking everything from vegetables and buttons to pots and pans up and down Chicago's congested streets, pushcart peddlers offered fellow immigrants necessities and familiar comforts. Evolving from sausages favored by European immigrants to the all-beef Vienna hot dogs popular today, the famed Chicago Dog became a pushcart fixture. Vendors, in penny-wise Jane Addams style, soon began adding salad mixtures on top to create meals in a bun for hungry customers. Although purists may protest, anything goes as you craft your own mini versions of Chicago's finest.

PREPARATION: 1 hour (45 minutes active)

½ cup diced pickled hot peppers

3 kosher dill pickle halves, diced

½ cup finely shredded Napa cabbage (or lettuce)

1 small white onion, minced

1–2 medium tomatoes, cored and seeds removed, finely diced

½ teaspoon celery salt

2 8-ounce packages of refrigerated seamless dough sheets

1 14-ounce package of mini all-beef frankfurters (40–42 mini hot dogs)

1 large egg

1 teaspoon poppy seeds

½ cup yellow mustard

1. Preheat the oven to 375 degrees.

2. Combine the peppers, pickles, cabbage, onion, tomatoes, and celery salt. Set aside this garden mixture for garnish.

3. Unroll an 8 x 12-inch refrigerated dough sheet onto a work surface. Press into a 10 x 12-inch rectangle. Cut the dough into 2-inch squares. Repeat with the second package of dough.

4. Place 1 mini frankfurter at the edge of a dough square and roll it up in the dough, pinching the seam of the dough together after you have finished rolling. Place the assembled frankfurters on the baking sheets seam side down. Using a paring knife, make a 1-inch incision lengthwise through the top of the dough and the frankfurter, taking care to leave ¼ inch intact at both ends of the hot dog and to cut only halfway down into the frankfurter. Repeat with the remaining frankfurters and dough.

5. Beat the egg with 1 tablespoon water and brush the tops of the mini dogs with the mixture. Sprinkle with the poppy seeds.

6. Bake 10 to 13 minutes, until slightly brown. Remove from the baking sheets and serve warm with the garden mixture and the mustard.

MULTI-BEAN SOUP

When Addams and her band of activists rang the dinner bell, they fed bodies and warmed hearts with family-style meals. Beans fill bellies and the steaming pots that emerged from the Hull-House kitchen did not disappoint. As a satisfying blend of comfort and practicality, soup hits the spot. Feel free to make bean substitutions—with thousands of bean varieties available, this soup can be customized to reflect your group's unique melting pot.

PREPARATION: 2 hours, 45 minutes, plus overnight (45 minutes active)

1 pound mixture of dried beans (navy, great northern, etc.), picked over and rinsed[1]

4 quarts cold water

¼ cup table salt

2 tablespoons olive oil

4 ounces pancetta or lean bacon, diced

1 cup chopped onion

2 large carrots, peeled and diced

1 tablespoon minced garlic

1 pound fresh mushrooms, quartered

2 quarts low-sodium chicken broth

1 14.5-ounce can diced tomatoes

2–3 bay leaves

½ teaspoon dried thyme

1 teaspoon pepper

Salt, to taste

---

1. Commercially available dried bean mixtures are readily obtainable if you prefer not to create your own mix. Just discard the flavor packet and use only the dried beans.

1. Place the dried beans in a pot with 4 quarts of cold water and the table salt. Cover and soak for 10 to 24 hours. Rinse thoroughly, drain, and set aside.

2. In a large pot, heat the olive oil over medium heat. Add the pancetta and cook until brown, 5 to 6 minutes. Add the onion and carrots and continue to cook 5 minutes more. Add the garlic and sauté briefly, then add the mushrooms and cook for 5 more minutes. When the mushrooms are softened and beginning to brown, pour in the chicken broth. Add the tomatoes and bring to a boil. Add the beans, bay leaves, thyme, pepper, and salt to taste. Partially cover the pot with a lid and simmer for 2 hours, or until the beans are tender. Discard the bay leaves before serving.

CHECKERBOARD COOKIES

Neapolitan ice cream, checkerboard cakes, and other trendy, patterned desserts emerged from late-nineteenth-century American kitchens. These checkerboard-design icebox cookies, tasty mirrors of Addams's crisscrossing cultures, put the wrap on your Hull-House evening.

PREPARATION: 2 hours, 15 minutes (30 minutes active)

3 cups all-purpose flour

1 cup nonfat dry milk powder

1 teaspoon baking powder

½ teaspoon salt

1 cup (2 sticks) unsalted butter, softened

1¾ cups sugar

1½ teaspoons vanilla

2 large eggs at room temperature, beaten

2 tablespoons Dutch-process cocoa

1. Sift together the flour, milk powder, baking powder, and salt.

2. Using an electric mixer, cream the butter until light in color. Add the sugar and continue to beat until fluffy. Add the vanilla and mix briefly. Add the eggs and beat until smooth. Slowly add the sifted dry ingredients and mix until just blended.

3. Place the dough on a work surface and divide in half. Knead the cocoa by hand into one of the halves.

4. Shape each half, the vanilla half and the cocoa half, into 2 x 2 x 9-inch rectangular blocks. Wrap each tightly in plastic wrap and chill until guests arrive (at least 45 minutes).

5. Unwrap the dough and with your guests' help, divide each block into 4 long 1 x 1 x 9-inch strips. First cut each block in half lengthwise, then lay each of the halves flat and cut them lengthwise in half again. You now have eight 1 x 1 x 9-inch rectangular strips, 4 vanilla and 4 chocolate. Keeping in mind the layout of a checkerboard, reassemble the strips together in a checkerboard pattern. Place a vanilla strip next to a chocolate strip on your work surface, then place a chocolate strip on top of the vanilla strip and a vanilla strip next to it, on top of the chocolate strip, to re-form one 2 x 2 x 9-inch rectangular block.

6. Repeat with the remaining 4 strips to reform the second checkerboard 2 x 2 x 9-inch block. Rewrap both blocks of dough and return to the refrigerator for 30 minutes, or until firm.

7. Preheat the oven to 350 degrees. Slice the dough blocks into ½-inch-thick squares and bake on ungreased baking sheets for 12 to 15 minutes, or until lightly browned. Allow cookies (approximately 36) to cool on baking sheet for five minutes before moving them to a wire rack.

CHICAGO TO GO

See the Robie House, designed by Frank Lloyd Wright, read Saul Bellow's *The Adventures of Augie March*, and recite poems by Gwendolyn Brooks and Carl Sandburg. . . . Revel in two of Wilco's musical collaborations: leader Jeff Tweedy's production of Mavis Staples's *You Are Not Alone*, and the band's celebration of Woody Guthrie, accompanied by Billy Bragg, on *Mermaid Avenue*, especially "Feed of Man.". . . Swap tales with columnist Mike Royko at the Billy Goat Tavern, "play two" with Ernie Banks at Wrigley Field, field grounders with Nellie Fox of the Go-Go Sox, watch Gale Sayers break tackles for the Bears and racial barriers with Brian Piccolo in *Brian's Song*. . . . Tour director John Hughes's hometown on *Ferris Bueller's Day Off,* watch Gary Sinese at Steppenwolf Theatre (once located in Hull-House), and read *August: Osage County* by Steppenwolf playwright Tracy Letts. . . . Sing along with Frank Sinatra that Chicago is "My Kind of Town," after spending a leisurely afternoon perusing the Art Institute. . . .

RESOURCES

PHILOSOPHY

Twenty Years at Hull-House by Jane Addams.

Peace and Bread in Time of War by Jane Addams.

MUSIC

Live by String Sisters: "Rumble Thy Bellyful."

Double Play by Liz Carroll and John Doyle: "A Pound a Week Rise."

At Newport 1960 by Muddy Waters: "I've Got My Mojo Working," "Baby, Please Don't Go."

Complete After Midnight Sessions by Nat King Cole: "(Get Your Kicks On) Route 66," "It's Only a Paper Moon."

Sun Rooms by Jason Adasiewicz: "Get in There."

Live at Carnegie Hall: 1938 by Benny Goodman: "Sing Sing Sing," "Avalon," "One O'Clock Jump."

The Imagine Project by Herbie Hancock: "Don't Give Up," "A Change Is Gonna Come."

Blowing in from Chicago by Clifford Jordan.

Definitive Buddy Guy by Buddy Guy: "First Time I Met the Blues," "Give Me My Coat and Shoes."

Earthshaker by Koko Taylor: "Let the Good Times Roll," "You Can Have My Husband," "Wang Dang Doodle."

FOOD

1896 Boston Cooking-School Cookbook by Fannie Merritt Farmer.

The Settlement Cook Book by Mrs. Simon Kander and Mrs. Henry Schoenfeld.

Simple Pleasures

MAY IN GREECE

I walked up a steep flight of steps to meet my host for a taped interview in which I thought (mistakenly) we would investigate a philosophical approach to good living. Friendly and agitated, fingering her marked-up copy of my book, she opened fire: "I really need to understand what you're *trying* to say in your chapter on simplicity. I always want more—more things, achievements, activities, more listeners, money. . . . Isn't that the American Dream? I like owning a spacious house and buying my kids the best sports equipment and trendy clothes. I drive a big car because I can afford it." She stopped. I had not started. Leaning back in her chair, she sighed and spoke slowly. "Sorry. I'm caught up in the whole consumer thing, but I see no way out and don't know if I would take it if I did. And it bothers me. You suggest that a simpler lifestyle frees us from clutter and the burden of possessions. It's crazy but I know that's true and still I don't believe it." Our interview ricocheted from topic to topic, always tumbling back to "your simplicity thing."

I'm not making light of her distress, because my well-intentioned host took her reading to heart and wrestled with the challenge to her lifestyle. She embodies the struggle most of us feel. We yearn to get down to basics in a world teeming with extras, but our knowing and our doing stretch miles apart. Her phone calls persisted until the day before the interview's airing: "Just want to be clear on a few things here. What am I supposed to do about my retirement plans? Do you recommend a garage sale or that I give things away? What will people think? Is a big income all right if you save the money?" I couldn't answer questions that belonged to her. I didn't listen to the broadcast because I was scared.

Philosophers, ancient and modern, Eastern and Western, agree. Things seduce and greed festers. Clever advertising succeeds with logos and brands lodging in memory. Accumulation *pre*-occupies us and detangling the knot is far from easy. I listened to an astonished mother's tale of her seven-year-old boy, heretofore happy in his passion for art and reading, lured into an enormous toy and candy store for a friend's birthday party. Confused and nervous, after thirty minutes he desperately wanted

some of everything. So fast! Young William's anxious reaction matches the radio host's dilemma—stuff surrounds us and its tug yanks hard.

What about the flower blooming through a tiny crack in the stone fence? How can we notice and appreciate *that*? Here's what I would have said to my radio host if an opening had appeared: We must work hard to make room for simple pleasures. We'll miss them, with noses pressed against store windows and fingers flipping through catalogs. Sometimes (most times?) the best buy is no buy. Our lives would simplify automatically if we thought hard about the ingredients of a happy life. Recognizing the essentials, we would then shoo away costly diversions.

I gratefully turn to my Haitian cab driver as powerful proof of the link between simple pleasures and happiness. After learning my destination, he asked me what brought me to New York. Quite briefly I explained my series of talks about the concepts at the core of good living. His animated questions and comments lifted my spirits for the duration of our all-too-short ride. At every stop, he made eye contact through the rearview mirror or turned to face me. I can still hear his voice. "It's the little things. It doesn't take much to be happy, like music and dancing. Knowing for sure that people love you and loving them back strong. Laughing and sitting around the dinner table telling stories. Helping people out and being welcome wherever you go. A few lazy days with your shoes off, perfect! Oh, yes, I love talking about all these pure pleasures." His joy rubbed off on me as he talked about friends "back home." Fumbling in my pockets for cash as the cab rolled to a slow stop, he faced me merrily and shared his last simple pleasure: "There is no charge, please. Our conversation makes me very happy."

I'll never forget my charioteer. New York City and its environs are home to some one hundred thousand Haitians. My cab ride occurred only a few days after the 2010 earthquake that left much of Haiti destroyed.

Though brokenhearted, he could still say, "There is no charge, please." He stands as a tall symbol for what philosophizing students long for—figuring out how to be in the midst of a busy world without losing sight of the ultimate prize. Ah! Intelligently picking and choosing basic and lasting pieces of happiness, unmoved by extravagance even while enjoying a fine meal and the long-anticipated vacation, staying on track despite the cry of the marketplace. The allure of possessions and the notion that more is better are old jokesters. The mall and a low interest rate scream at us. But we can rise above the noise and refurbish our lives with clear-headed priorities. Think of survivors of earthquakes, tornadoes, floods, illness, loss. What do they remind us each time? My college friend Betsy finds her words as she describes her husband's response to cancer: "People often ask how Jay maintains his grace and humor in the face of the storm. He finds the beauty in every moment. With illness every moment clearly becomes precious and there is plenty of beauty waiting to be revealed. Sometimes it takes a storm to wake us up to what has been right in front of us all along. It's a practice that only needs to be activated." Don't we all know this, deep down? Must we discover the value of simple pleasures the hard way?

Child philosophers convince me that we can learn our lessons more easily. In the middle of a thoughtful circle of fourth graders, surrounded by eavesdropping teachers and parents, we thought hard together about what's necessary for a happy life. "Freedom, peace, deep breaths, love, playtime, flowers, comforting words, learning something new. . . ." After forty taller and shorter philosophers had spoken, I wondered aloud if anyone noticed something that all their choices shared. Hands shot up. "Nobody mentioned 'stuff' unless it was important, like clean water, a roof, and clothes right for the weather." Grown-ups nodded in wistful agreement. So the question remains for all ages: How do we remember

our basic hunger for the "soul food" that simple pleasures satisfy? How can we "activate the practice," as Betsy says?

The child philosophers answer. "I will keep telling myself that I only have one life . . . take time every day to walk and listen . . . practice putting what's important first . . . give my mind a second chance whenever I forget . . . think deep down and let my understanding soak in . . . and trust myself to be smart."

Let's set sail for Athens where a garden of simple pleasures blooms. Epicurus (eh-pih-KYOOR-us) trusts us to be smart, too. He whispers an enticing proposal: If you walk carefully and quickstep around the pitfall of desire, simple pleasures will sweep you off your feet.

PREPPING FOR GREECE

Dance with Anthony Quinn in Mihalis Kakogiannis's film *Zorba the Greek* and practice your moves to "Zorba's Dance" with the soundtrack composed by legendary Mikis Theodorakis. . . . Set sail from Piraeus for some island-hopping: First stop the craggy isle of Santorini to lounge on the beach and tour the village of Oia, onward to Samos, Epicurus's first home, to give a long look at the famed Eupalinian aqueduct and the capital city of Vathy, and restfully extend your stay on Crete, with its rich history and the marvels of ancient Minoan civilization. . . . Stand with the gods and goddesses of mythology on Mount Olympus, check out The School of Philosophy at Aristotle University in Thessaloniki, parade through the gates and imagine the participants in the first Games held in Olympia, admire a marble copy of Myron's Bronze Age sculpture of the "Discobolos" and feel the power of the discus thrower. . . . Watch *Dogtooth*, directed by Yorgos Lanthimos and add *A Touch of Spice* with Fanis and his grandpa in Tassos Boulmetis's film. . . .

WE WILL LEAVE LIFE CRYING ALOUD IN A GLORIOUS TRIUMPH-SONG THAT WE HAVE LIVED WELL.

EPICURUS,
Fragments

Imagine swing dancing in a circling chorus belting out such a "triumph-song"! How can we look back at our lives with joy in our very bones that we got it right? Can we warm to the world and swallow its beauty whole? Will we remember how to relish pleasure while avoiding the painful repercussions of excess? Yes, Epicurus answers, inviting us into his quiet community. Polishing our skill of anticipation, we can predict with growing precision the consequences of our actions. New and experienced philosophers of all ages gravitate to the plain words of this Greek gardener. He gives each of us the opportunity of becoming the teller of our own fortunes. Accepting his offer of a "feast of preserved cheese" (*Fragments*), we rediscover the sweet satisfaction of life's simple pleasures.

CONSEQUENCE

The reluctance to think about the consequences of our choices, and the difficulty in doing so when we try, is as old as any human weakness. Desire nabs those who let down their guard. Retreating from political turmoil and the strife of competition, Epicurus opened his self-sustaining commune outside Athens twenty-five hundred years ago. The unquestioned habit of wanting new and more, of longing for "dainties" (*Fragments*), surrounded him as it does us. One annual event offers glaring testimony of today's consumer mindset. What drives potential customers who stake out places in lengthening lines at 4:00 a.m. on the Friday after Thanksgiving, jockeying for position and readying for the charge when doors fling open? Tired and irritated, Thursday's pumpkin pie barely digested, what are we doing?

Epicurus responds by covering each of our faces with a thin veil. What happens? The world warps when observed through this gauzy film—reality becomes fuzzy and disconcerting. It is with this symbolic gesture that Epicurus delivers the heart of his message. Illusions pass for truth in a mind swamped by desire. Under the spell of want, unable to find our way, we steer far from life's lasting pleasures and plunge into a jungle of trouble. Let's follow Epicurus's path out of the haze. Flushing out illusions and staring them down, we can regain our grasp on reality.

Tempting us with a crusty piece of bread and a cup of cool water, Epicurus holds up a gold coin glinting in the sunlight, highlighting our biggest mistake. Money acquires value for its own sake, posing as life's ultimate goal and the measuring rod of success. The workforce shoves us from behind and propels us forward into ever more furiously paced days and short, edgy nights. How many of us does Epicurus rightly recognize as "involved too deeply in the business of some occupation" (*Fragments*)? Here we are, heads stuck in briefcases, eyes glued to computer spreadsheets, ears perked up for the sale, and mouths watering at the dangle of a fat bonus.

Danger straight ahead!

Epicurus reminds us: Realize the dire consequences of confusing the long-term goal of a pleasurable life with the short-term objective of moneymaking. Hold tight the knowledge that peace of mind evaporates when money and work are mistaken for the good life. The gold coin can buy the things you *want*, but will it purchase what you truly *need*? And so long as we travel along the money trail, we can guarantee ourselves "rest stagnant and activity mad" (*Fragments*) while life's basic beauties lie hidden.

Resting in the shade of a big-branching tree, Epicurus forces us to face another money-made error. This look in the mirror hurts. I've convinced myself that I can conquer insecurity and worry if I accumulate a stockpile of things. Satisfying desires, especially epi curiously described "vain fancies," shields me from hard times and others' disapproval. No sacrifice is too great if it buys me a sense of achievement. But look at the frightful consequence when I wear my financial status like protective armor—I depend on money and possessions to give my life meaning. What I own defines me. Ugh. This cycle spins like a dervish, never letting up. Craving spirals out of control unless quenched. What utter foolishness for me to think that material possessions can shield me from heartache and pain. I know that pleasure in ownership is fleeting. Gadgets and toys break, cruises and parties end. Yet the chase intensifies. What happens if I lose what I have? Just a quick glance around my town confirms Epicurus's forecast. Why does the storage shed business boom? What fiscal folly left the skeletal scar of a foreclosed luxury hotel looming above the city's skyline? How can a college allow representatives of credit card companies to set up shop outside the library(!), barking their offers of "no interest" and free pizza to young, uninformed students? Listen to this (almost) hilarious description of a credit/debit card, shared by a kindergartener with a classmate: "Did you know there are these thin pieces of plastic that make money pop out of a machine? Do you think the money is real?" They looked my way: "Do you?" What a tough question!

There's no mistaking Epicurean common sense. "Every desire must be confronted by this question: What will happen to me if the object of my desire is accomplished and what if it is not" (*Fragments*)? That's the point. Pleasure is *the* good, but only if its consequences aren't wrapped in mental anguish. The worst result of our greedy appetites should sadden us all. We overlooked myriad, readily available simple pleasures, missed out on pain-free joys that last a lifetime, and our store-bought happiness still eludes us. The question now hovers over us. Will we use our new understanding and make pure pleasure ours? Talk means nothing unless we act on our insights. "We must laugh and philosophize at the same time" (*Fragments*) and get on with the search for good living.

TRUTH

It's time for each of us individually to put philosophy to work. While I deal with my bad habits and you with yours, the rallying cry "Cut it out!" unites us. While delving into this honest examination of the consumer way, Epicurus first offers the two seemingly cost-free indulgences of procrastination and gossip as further evidence of the damage that lurks within unforeseen consequences. Neither procrastination nor gossip provides pleasure, but if shortsighted we fall under their sway. Anticipate. The procrastinator manufactures anxiety. Due dates for stacks of bills loom—and pass. When I refuse another call from my tenant, the pipe bursts. Frequent laments that "I know your syllabus states 'no late papers' but I've never written any other kind" reveal one more startled student connection between delay and misfortune. Anticipate. The office gossip, delighting in manipulation, uncovers misery when truth surfaces. His rumor-spreading costs him trust and friendship at the office and on the team. Anticipate. "I get it!" enthusiastic diners respond to these obvious examples. More pleasure comes *my* way if I defeat my old stalling tactics or I promote goodwill rather than hurtful hearsay. Similarly, when I stand guard over the consequences of my habitual buying, the thicket of things thins out, little by lot, and I find my way. Passing up the bargain on a power tool that I'll add to my shelves of unused gizmos . . . winning out over the online gaming obsession that cost me sleep and a girlfriend . . . admitting that

I require only one tennis racquet to hit the ball . . . noticing the purchases still in unopened bags . . . confessing that just one set of sheets makes a bed. . . .

Yes, we get it. By cutting back on accumulation, like clipping back a rosebush, we allow for new growth. Unburdened by clutter, we feel a rather wondrous sense of independence emerge. Epicurus salutes freedom from worry as "the greatest of riches" (*Fragments*) bought by mind's victory over matter. Better at anticipating consequences, we purchase self-reliance and security as we streamline our lives. Epicurus proves right again in his faith that nature "has made what is necessary easy to supply, and what is not (easy) unnecessary" (*Fragments*). In the current economic swoon, a financial adviser takes great pleasure when she hears clients repeatedly acknowledge how little money it takes to live well. Repair businesses thrive. Clear-cut living buys time. Hassle no longer sells.

Ah. We learn again or find anew what

feeds our spirit, celebrating our talents while sharing our happiness. When he blows on that pocket piano, Kevin's long love affair with his harmonica makes merriment for all. Reviving his youthful love of theater, the book editor's performance as Shakespeare's Polonius brings down the house. Possibilities abound for learning a new language . . . awaking at dawn for a run . . . digging in the dirt or whittling wood . . . tracing imagination on a sketch pad . . . taking the first steps in salsa dancing . . . playing catch and telling tales . . . watching a cloud separate into butterfly's wings and observing the icicle's slow drip . . . bumping knees while huddled over a card game . . . caressing your first grown-up wallet, barely poking through its mending wad of tape. Taking flat-out pleasure in what my mother calls a "spoonable day," good enough to eat—how about that?

More Epicurean rewards spill out. As gratitude for simple pleasures fills and fuels us, the habit of need shrinks naturally. Hearts open as stores empty. Giving provides tremendous joy. Susan, whose passion consists in caring for abandoned dogs, explains: "It's complete satisfaction knowing that I'm giving another being everything in my power." Epicurus concurs that "the wise man knows better how to give than to receive" (*Fragments*). It's the "ungrateful greed of the soul" (*Fragments*) that ruins us. And friendship, Epicurus's premier pleasure, requires only the free gift of our time. Friendship strengthens, lightens, and restores. It bolsters confidence during difficulty. "Friendship goes dancing around the world proclaiming to us all to awake to the praises of a happy life" (*Fragments*). As time passes, bountiful "grateful recollections" (*Fragments*) lie in memory's vault at our fingertips. For Epicurus, and he predicts for us, also, this treasure trove never runs out. Memory trumps sadness and a shared reminiscence consoles grieving storytellers.

Epicurus's philosophy comes to us mostly from letters written to his companions. A last letter instructed his friends "to give all the books that belong to me to Hermarchus" (*Fragments*). Pleases me every time.

~~~~~~~~~~~~~~~~~~~~~~~~~~~~~~~~~~~~

AND YOUR TOPIC FOR DINNER CONVERSATION IS

Epicurus issues a bold challenge: "We must concern ourselves with the healing of our own lives" (*Fragments*). Do you find the prospect of healing from the haze of material preoccupations attractive? How can you become more the philosopher and less a consumer? What simple steps can you take to loosen the hold of material possessions? Describe a wise person's priorities. (*You* are the "wise person!")

~~~~~~~~~~~~~~~~~~~~~~~~~~~~~~~~~~~~

THE DOORBELL RINGS

Guests' choices range among a variety of tasty possibilities. For starters, perhaps Agrinion (jumbo green) and Kalamata (black) olives, dried figs, and nuts. Maybe pick up a bottle of ouzo for a robust toast? Stuffed grape leaves, or *dolmades*, available in many groceries, provide a distinctive addition. Room-temperature retsina, a rustic Greek white or rosé wine flavored with pine resin, nicely complements tonight's recipes. With a quick stop at a commercial bakery, two guests can treat the group to dessert with baklava (layered filo pastry with nuts and honey) and *kourambiethes* (traditional Greek shortbread cookies).

Meet "The White Rose of Athens," Nana Mouskouri, as you gather when "Day Is Done." For five decades to global delight, she sang the soul of Greece in many languages with an intimacy flavored by the long history of the Greek islands. When she asks "Why Worry?" you won't! George Dalaras comes to the party *Live and Unplugged*, singing "Dui Dui." Though he entertained the masses in a packed Athens Olympic Stadium, tonight his intimate phrasing and tone, embodying the bluesy emotion of *rembetiko* artists, belong to you. Using ouzo glasses and a tabletop to tap along to the lively beat, *rembetiko* fans flock to local *ouzeries* to raise a glass and participate in this underground blues tradition. From the plentiful ouzo poured in these uniquely Greek taverns, to the artisanal ouzo still produced on the island of Lesvos, using anise and other sweet-smelling herbs, the country's most popular drink has a devoted following. If your guests indulge in small glasses of this powerful spirit, keep the appetizers coming! Dalaras's fellow *rembetiko* artist Vassilis Tsitsanis's sad "Synefiasmeni Kyriaki" ("Cloudy Sunday") marks the occupation of his beloved Greece. Listen at least twice to one of his country's best-known songs as you make your move from kitchen to conversation.

Vangelis softens the mood, alone and then with a special friend. This child composer grew up to write the score for the film *Chariots of Fire*. Enjoy especially, but not only, the well-known title track. Next, the inimitable voice of Irene Papas meshes with Vangelis's arrangements of traditional Greek folk songs, and the evocation of simpler times blends nicely with your discussion. Float down "Le Fleuve" ("The River") as Papas celebrates "swirl, beat, and wave." Yanni's elegant piano compositions performed *Live at the Acropolis* serve as a perfect background for the heart of your talk. Dream yours as Yanni performs "One Man's Dream." As your conversation winds down, opera star Agnes Baltsa, lending her soaring soprano to *Songs My Country Taught Me*, paints simple pleasures in sound with "Áspri Méra Ke Ya Mas."

Is it time to go, so soon? Wait long enough to "Look at the Night!" with Haris Alexiou and drink small cups of strong Greek coffee. Can you spot "Siva's Moon Dance," captured on the jazzy sitar strings pinched by Nana Simopoulos?

LAMB MEATBALLS WITH PITA WEDGES AND TZATZIKI

Epicurus's distaste for dining alone was shared by countrymen who relished vigorous conversation around a festive banquet table. Plato adored figs, Homer called for "stronger wine," and Plutarch cautioned against individual portions because they "killed sociability" (*The Philosopher's Kitchen*). The ancient Greek tradition of nourishing both mind and body also sustains the modern communal table. Called *meze*, the small dishes shared today are not intended to sate the appetite. Instead, passing these simple plates of food provides pleasurable bite-size morsels for diners at gatherings large and small. Lamb, traditionally featured at Greek feasts, is a mainstay of the popular Greek wrap, or gyro, but can be replaced in this tasty *meze* with your choice of ground meat.

LAMB MEATBALLS

PREPARATION: 1 hour

2 teaspoons olive oil

½ cup finely chopped onion

3 cloves garlic, peeled and minced

2 pounds ground lamb (or a combination of ground beef and lamb, or ground chicken, etc.)

2 large eggs, beaten

½ cup whole milk

½ cup plain dried breadcrumbs (panko style preferred)

Grated zest from 1–2 lemons

1 tablespoon dried oregano

1 teaspoon salt

½ teaspoon pepper

2 tablespoons butter

2 tablespoons olive oil

1. Preheat the oven to 450 degrees.

2. Heat the 2 teaspoons olive oil in a medium pan over medium heat. When shimmering, add the onion and sauté for 1 to 2 minutes. Add the garlic and continue to sauté for 1 to 2 minutes more, until the mixture is softened but not brown. Set aside to cool.

3. In a large bowl, combine the lamb, eggs, milk, breadcrumbs, zest, oregano, salt,

pepper, and the cooled onion and garlic. Mix until blended. Form the mixture into 1½-inch balls.

4. Line two rimmed baking sheets with aluminum foil. Put 1 tablespoon of the butter and 1 tablespoon of the olive oil on each sheet and heat in the oven just until the butter melts. Be careful not to let it burn.

5. Arrange the meatballs on the baking sheets (making sure they do not touch) and return the pans to the oven. Reduce the oven temperature to 350 degrees.

6. Bake the meatballs for 10 minutes. Use tongs to turn the meatballs, then continue to bake for 10 more minutes, or until nicely browned and cooked through.

7. Alternatively, heat the 2 tablespoons olive oil in a large pan over medium-high heat and sauté the meatballs in batches, adding additional olive oil as needed (you won't use the butter). Do not crowd the meatballs in the pan or they will not brown and will become soggy. The meatballs are ready when they are nicely browned, and cooked through, about 15 minutes.

8. Serve hot with the tzatziki and the pita wedges.

TZATZIKI

PREPARATION: 2 hours, 15 minutes
(15 minutes active)

1 16-ounce container of plain Greek-style yogurt

2–3 cloves garlic, minced

1 large cucumber, peeled, seeded, and minced

1 tablespoon extra virgin olive oil

1½ tablespoons white vinegar, plus more to taste

½ teaspoon salt, plus more to taste

Pita wedges, for serving

1. Place all the ingredients in a small bowl and combine. Adjust the salt and vinegar if desired.

2. Chill for 2 hours.

BARLEY WITH CURRANTS, PINE NUTS, AND FETA

Little is known about specific foods grown in Epicurus's garden, but the philosopher was reputed to eat a largely grain-based diet, flavored with occasional dried berries, nuts, and cheese. This recipe combines those simple ingredients—barley, currants, pine nuts, and feta—that the Greeks have enjoyed since the days of antiquity.

Declared by Homer in *The Odyssey* to be the "marrow of men," barley appears in ancient vase paintings. Cultivated and sundried on hillsides surrounding the ancient city of Corinth, currants—often called Corinthian raisins—were eaten alone as dessert or incorporated into fancy, celebratory dishes. Harvested from stone pine trees and believed by Poseidon to be sacred because they grew on craggy cliffs next to the sea, pine nuts were often preserved in honey. The salty and slightly sour taste of feta, a sheep or goat's milk cheese cut into cubes and aged in brine-filled barrels, drops you on Aegean shores.

PREPARATION: 45 minutes (15 minutes active)

4 quarts water

2 cups pearled barley

2½ teaspoons salt

¾ cup dried currants

½ cup pine nuts

1–2 tablespoons fresh lemon juice

1 tablespoon honey

½ cup extra virgin olive oil

¾ cup thinly sliced scallions

½ cup crumbled feta cheese

1. Bring 4 quarts of water to a boil in a medium pot over high heat. Add the barley and 2 teaspoons of the salt, reduce the heat, and simmer for 25 to 30 minutes, until the barley is tender. Drain the barley in a colander.

2. Place the currants in a small bowl and cover with boiling water. Let sit 3 to 5 minutes to plump. Drain and set aside.

3. Heat the pine nuts in a dry skillet over medium-low heat until fragrant, 5 to 10 minutes. Stir frequently.

4. To make the dressing, mix the lemon juice with the remaining ½ teaspoon salt in a small bowl. Stir in the honey until combined. Drizzle in the olive oil, whisking to incorporate.

5. In a medium-sized serving bowl, combine the barley, currants, pine nuts, and scallions. Add the dressing and stir. Sprinkle the feta on top and toss briefly.

GREECE TO GO

Listen to Cream's vocal tribute to the "Tales of Brave Ulysses," and to Michalis Terzis plucking the strings of his pear-shaped instrument, showcasing the *Magic of the Greek Bouzouki: Near the Sea.* . . . Read a chapter of Homer's *The Iliad* or *The Odyssey* complemented by poems from sixth-century B.C.E. lyricist Sappho. . . . Tour the Acropolis and uncover the prophecy that the surprised philosopher Socrates learned from the Oracle at Delphi, drop by the Parthenon and, leaning against a big rock, picture a dramatic performance at the Theater of Dionysus of Sophocles's *Antigone* or Euripides's *Trojan Women*. . . . Read Nikos Kazantzakis's irresistible *Zorba the Greek*, join Melina Mercouri in her romp through life in Jules Dassin's

Never on Sunday, humming the theme on Monday, and dedicate time to a performance recorded live of any aria sung by the inimitable soprano Maria Callas, La Divina. . . .

RESOURCES

PHILOSOPHY

Epicurus: The Extant Remains by Epicurus, translated by Cyril Bailey. (Referred to as *Fragments* in the text.)

MUSIC

Only Love by Nana Mouskouri: "Why Worry."

Passport by Nana Mouskouri: "The White Rose of Athens," "Day Is Done."

Live and Unplugged by George Dalaras: "Dui Dui."

Rembetika 4: The Postwar Years—CD C: 1947–1950 by Vassilis Tsitsanis: "Synefiasmeni Kyriaki" ("Cloudy Sunday").

Chariots of Fire by Vangelis: "Titles."

Odes by Irene Papas: "Le Fleuve" ("The River").

Live at the Acropolis by Yanni: "One Man's Dream."

Songs My Country Taught Me by Agnes Baltsa: "Áspri Méra Ke Ya Mas."

Anthology by Haris Alexiou: "Look at the Night!"

Daughters of the Sun by Nana Simopoulos: "Siva's Moon Dance."

FOOD

The Philosopher's Kitchen: Recipes from Ancient Greece and Rome for the Modern Cook by Francine Segan.

Meze: Small Plates to Savor and Share from the Mediterranean Table by Diane Kochilas.

The Odyssey by Homer.

History of Greek Food (blog) by Mariana Kavroulaki. historyofgreekfood.org

Liberating Education

JUNE IN BRAZIL

One telling tale unfurls inside another. Sipping tea with students and townsfolk at an Ivy League university, our conversation about the rewards of sharing philosophy with children elicits anecdotes and remembrances of youthful wisdom. In this lighthearted atmosphere I related the following story, drawn from my experience with child philosophers. . . .

I always ask children, at some point in my time with them, to tell me why they are in school. Their reactions and responses are predictable. Eyes narrow with misgiving, heads turn for reassurance that no one has an answer, and faces convey their doubts as to why *I* am in *their* school. For once no hands shoot up right away. Nothing keeps happening, so I repeat the request. Come on, you spend six hours a day in this building, five days a week, lug heavy backpacks aboard the bus, complete homework assignments . . . and you can't tell me why? Inevitably, when a child ventures an answer, it's a variation of "I'm in school to get a job." We laugh together when I ask them what jobs are available for eight-year-olds, and then we devote time to the first of our ongoing discussions about the value of education. Children find the prospects of owning their educations appealing. "I can go my way." "I'll know how to protect myself." "Hey! School is my job. Don't need another one yet." Kaboom! The second story unleashes. . . .

My first nor'easter! Winds of rising voices sweep through the staid room as college students speak excitedly, simultaneously, amazed in their agreement that ownership of their *own* education is for most a spanking new concept. A third-year student sits on the edge of her chair, staring past me, her hand repeatedly going up but immediately falling back into her lap. Finally she speaks: "Sorry, but the idea that my education belongs to me makes me dizzy. The purpose of school for me since kindergarten was to attend this university. I feel bullied by the whole experience. It's sad that I'm shocked by what should not be a novel concept but it's wild to think of making my education mine." The pot stirred, from afternoon tea through a leisurely dinner we poked at education. Students talked about their journeys and asked me to describe my classroom at a community college. I offered them this narrative peek at a typical first day: I wonder, as usual, why so many prospective students look downcast and resigned on day one. Their heaviness prompts me to ask why they aren't enthusiastic and who told them education was a drag. I use their surprised silence as a chance to tell them that I intend to learn and enjoy myself, that every student makes my knowledge of tattered texts new, that sitting in a circle, we will know each other's names and more—I insist that they question the relevance and accuracy of everything we read and continually reassess the value of the course itself. When students note on the syllabus that they design their own tests and/or paper topics, some grin at the anticipated easy A, while others correctly spot the challenge.

I replied to the Ivy Leaguers' curiosity about such "out of the box" academic freedom with assurance that the quality of student work soars with students' autonomy.

My freed pupils figure it out: "I really had to read and reread to come up with a topic, but the trick worked and I was proud of my paper." "If you don't know the material really well you can't make up a test; I was nervous on the due date and I was taking my own exam!" "First time I ever used 'I' in a paper, and I got it right!"

Children entering the workforce and college students startled by school—time to rethink *education*, a word that's been bandied about with little question as to its meaning. Why and how to become an educated person? I always return to the Latin source of the word for help in renewing my grasp of the essence of education. The root of *education* suggests a process of bringing forward, leading up, drawing out. I picture individuals climbing a steep hill together, teachers and students in spry pursuit of knowledge. The word conveys positive images, this movement "forward, up, and out" so we can stand on higher ground.

Because we educate ourselves every day with what we read, hear, study, and watch, we should grab the controls. Dining philosophers heartily investigate how they know what they know, an especially pertinent inquiry in the "information age." Bombarded by constant sound bites and instant newsfeeds, how do we know what's true? Dinner companions never run out of examples: newspapers print "corrections and retractions" at least a day later, headlines switch the same event into strangely different stories, history books are removed from public schools due to inaccuracies, we seek second and tenth opinions in medical diagnoses. Diners determine to develop more solid and sure sources of information, educating themselves "broad" and "deep."

If we free the concept of education from negativity, education of all kinds frees us. Meet four liberated students and taught teachers. Final exam for ethics class produces two very different successes. First: The smell of fresh glue binds a handmade supplemental text for our class, with articles on unexplored topics arranged in chapters, and an excellent student presents his customary superior work. Second: A still-shy but newly self-possessed young woman appears at my door. Attending every class yet missing every assignment, she won't pass the course. "I can't write, so I made a Power-Point presentation for us to watch. That way I can show you what I've learned." She talked. I choked up. Not only did she grasp every ethical issue explored in class but also, "I know what I want. I'm a certified nursing assistant, love my patients, and learn so much from them. I don't mind bedpans or training sessions. I learned from this class that it's my life and school may not be for me." She strides away with a victorious swish. Now a fact-fueled seventh grader tells the principal that "we should not be celebrating Columbus Day. It's wrong." Finally, a retired newsman greets his pupil with his carefully prepared assignments and gifts of grammar books. If (when) she receives her general equivalency diploma, a life presents itself for her and her son. Glued books, superb "failing" work, a child's private research, a reporter gently stopping his soon bilingual pupil at her every made-up word. . . . Smell the fresh air.

Education never ends. Want to invent and reinvent your lifelong educational prospects? A Brazilian soccer and samba fan proclaims that "to converse with people is a way to read the world. I love to eat . . . and I need to eat with other people" (*The Politics of Education*). Set a place for passionate educator Paulo Freire (POW-lo freh-EE-reh). Getting smart over lively, music-backed dinner conversation? This philosopher is our guy.

PREPPING FOR BRAZIL

Move to *Jazz Samba* by Charlie Byrd and Stan Getz, down the field with soccer greats Marta, Pelé, and Neymar, and move even faster at the first beat of Tropicália in Os Mutantes's "Baby. . . ." Learn about the careers and philanthropic legacies of racecar driver Ayrton Senna and pianist/composer João Carlos Martins. . . . Tour the *Amazon* in Kieth Merrill's documentary, exploring the Amazon River Delta and its lush biodiversity, returning to the rainforest to taste the açaí berry, attend the opera at the Teatro Amazonas in Manaus, and walk along Alter do Chão's river beaches in Pará. . . . Delight in the performance of Fernanda Montenegro in Walter Salles's film *Central do Brasil* (*Central Station*), root for children pulled out of the Maré *favela* ("slum") into Luta Pela Paz ("Fight for Peace") as they throw punches to music in *capoeira* and develop computer and citizenship skills. . . . Stroll through São Paulo's Ibirapuera Park and duck into the Museum of Modern Art, research inspirational environmentalist and union leader Chico Mendes, and welcome your introduction to the music of Leny Andrade and Eliane Elias. . . .

THE FIRST THING I MUST SAY ABOUT WHAT I LIKE TO DO IS I LIKE TO LIVE!

PAULO FREIRE,
The Politics of Education

From the days of his impoverished youth through years of exile in Chile, Africa, and the United States, Freire's "belief in a permanent search for knowledge" (*Politics*) directed his every move. Focusing first and always on the unacceptable illiteracy of the Brazilian peasantry, his educational approach won international applause and wide application. Twentieth-century professor of education and rebel philosopher, in tent wanderer in a big city or at the beach, Freire lived learning. No friend of the status quo—and champion of everyone's intellectual ability—he rebels against any limit imposed on the liberating power of education. We'll labor with him in the pits of educational malpractice and then revel in the heady atmosphere of the real thing.

STALE

Our look at wrongheaded education begins with the memory of a long-ago youthful pastime that serves as an unfortunate analogy for bad educational practice. A child drops a coin in a penny bank, the adolescent continues putting away deposits, and the adult accumulates a full container—but the money is counterfeit! Likewise an oppressive educational system stuffs unwary students' heads with information that serves only the ruling society's best interests. Like phony money, students can't use this information, either. The brain-bank jammed, the mind holds no room for any knowledge that matches an individual's life experience. There are no tools handed out for forging a better life, combating inequity, or maximizing potential. Pennies of faux learning saved, but none worth spending. The "banking method anesthetizes" submissive students and hides a world "undergoing constant transformation" (*Pedagogy of the Oppressed*). The world is set and everyone's place dictated and ensured by mass education. Dates memorized. Conquests chronicled. Financiers admired. Generals serenaded. Another mouth and case closed. Disrespected students can count on regular deposits for guidance through adulthood, "acting according to the prescriptions they receive daily from the communications media . . . there is always some manual that says what to do" (*Politics*). Every thought standardized, each individual subdued, one more life stopped in its proper tracks.

No happenstance involved here. "Society molds education to conform to those values that sustain it" so that schooling "benefits those in power" (*Politics*). Children, college students, and roundtable philosophers attest to the damage inflicted by this practice. Children shut up and shut down. "I was drawing feelings about my hard life but the teacher tore it up and made me trace a snowman . . . in August!" College students protect grades by returning the expected dividends on deposits plunked into their heads by bankers/teachers. Psychology tests consist of true or false and multiple-choice questions. A philosophy graduate student recounts receiving an A minus on her first paper with no written comment whatsoever, and when asked, the professor responded that "there's nothing wrong with it, but that's not the way we do it here." Diners speak out against twelve years of school in which, "No one ever, once, asked me what I thought." "I was a number, never a name." Far from Freire's goal of problem posing and solving education, we suffocate.

Woe.

Stamped with society's approval, this dominant "class knowledge" successfully devalues other kinds of intelligence. Understanding this one definite body of knowledge secures rank. But education happens outside the classroom and learning occurs far from school. Tales of malfeasance erupt around dinner tables. A loving couple, a plumber and a professor, combats ridicule. The snobbish blue collar/white collar distinction humiliates as the ashamed handyman and day care worker mumble when asked about their occupations.

Jean puts down her fork and channels Freire's spirit. "All knowledge matters. Freire mastered the intricacies of Portuguese. He's part of the educational system and wants it to work. I still take classes. But Freire coaxes us to learn it All. As I get older I feel less educated. Can't fix my car, grow food, build shelter, and until our first dinner, I puzzled about what 'vegetables and fruits in season' might mean. Aren't tomatoes always *there*? If trouble comes and electricity goes, all eyes will be on the farmer, carpenter, herbalist, and outdoors people. What's edible, where, how to fix it?"

Isn't it possible to combine "formal education" and "informal knowledge" (*Letters to Cristina*)? Can't Jean spend time perusing the library *and* staking tomato plants? What knowledge can the concert performer glean from her deaf piano tuner? "No one gets from one side of the street to the other without crossing it" (*Politics*). Look both ways. Let's cross.

FRESH

Stories are us. They are not *about* our lives, they *are* our lives. Dialogue personalizes education for all involved, and "education . . . will be more rewarding if it stimulates the development of this radical, human need for expression. . . . Creative and communicative language" (*Politics*) forms the bedrock of the learning process. Verbal exchanges position individuals in charge of their educations, anywhere, at any age. We discover truths in conversation that quite often remain obscure to the solitary thinker.

Although that "bank" and the media pound away, Freire's demand for dialogue

lives! Paulo, meet your dinner partners, models of spirited philosophical dialogue. A stylish woman approaching ninety woos the Vietnam veteran, hairdresser, and chiropractor as she tells tales of her mother's Great Depression survival skills and her own wartime nursing career. Stockbroker and electrician trade (honest) tips; sculptor and dermatologist describe skin texture; city council member and high school coach analyze "a sentence in the newspaper, a political speech" (*Politics*); librarian jots down book titles suggested by occupational therapist and journalist; actor and bistro server talk about pleasing their clienteles. Freire lifts a glass as "knowledge emerges through . . . continuing, hopeful inquiry . . . in the world, with the world, with each other" (*Pedagogy*).

Professor Freire, welcome to these classrooms. Ethics students close books and prepare food to exact specifications for dinner with AIDS patients. Unforgettable narratives spun around the table teach big lessons better than any book. A pupil politely challenges the history professor about the accuracy of his lectures glamorizing the "settlement" of America, embodying Freire's plea that "it is most necessary to doubt" (*Politics*). A former dropout commands classmates to keep up with their reading, chiding them to "teach me, offend me, startle me!" Conflicting accounts of a military operation deploy teacher and students on a truth-seeking mission, reporting back at the beginning of the next class. Faculty members encourage a young woman to quit school for a year and forget her academic study of the music industry, encouraging her traveling internship with a band. A volunteer consultant teaches kids and staff in the public schools about nutrition, choosing local foods, and cutting costs, reminiscent of Freire's critical boyhood lessons in picking papayas at the moment of ripening. Relevant, problem-solving education manifests in small hands grabbing black bean and brown rice tacos from the cafeteria line, pre-paring and eating a helping from a hummus and vegetable plate, and crunching on a granola snack.

Andy, thank your Brazilian mentor. Andy's fourth-year students must apply for his course in which they hash out the classics of Russian literature with residents at a juvenile correctional facility. Exposed to real-life problems, flipping through pages in *Crime and Punishment*, they seek solutions together. Relationships cement. Stereotypes shatter. Andy gains new insights behind bars about his field of study and the residents, who are "emotive, complex, and even humorous," often making the most obvious connections that no one else saw. University students discover that "literature changes us" and isn't the exclusive property of "the critics." Residents participate in an educational practice that works in their best interests, which bodes well for continued study. After the semester ends, three musically talented residents work on a rock rendition of their favorite Russian short stories,

stories that taught them to "love my life." Freire might smile at his memory of a student so moved by *Pedagogy of the Oppressed* that he set it to music.

Freire lights a fire around dinner tables, chairs tipped on front legs as sitters put their heads together. Anyone teaching anything reconsiders their approach—the ESL teacher rethinks what books might better relate to her pupils' lives, and the administrator fumbles for fixes within the current educational system, looking to Finland for possible improvements. Suggestions emerge for being better informed about political candidates: follow the money trail, detect traces of corporate involvement, and distinguish between straightforward statements and sleight-of-mouth distortions by being "ready not to accept what is said just because it is said" (*Politics*). In the age of nonstop electronic blasts, helpful tips in pursuit of accuracy surface: A war veteran listened to both an English translation of Al Jazeera news broadcasts and military intelligence when stationed in Baghdad, and put together pieces of the puzzle as best he could, prompting other diners to tune in to international broadcasts and seek out renegade journalism. Checking out a blogger's publications and affiliations and knowing who owns a newspaper or network matters. And what advice does Freire offer his readers? "Start rereading this book. I am inviting my readers to act as subjects and thus to reject the idea of merely accepting my analysis" (*Politics*).

The diverse embrace of Freire's educational approach comes as no surprise. What a vivifying tonic, drunk by—among many others—museum curators, mathematicians, scientists, sociologists, theologians, anthropologists, musicians, philosophers, and educators. Freire especially appreciated the use of his work by anyone trying to understand better the political underpinnings of their own country. "Back in Brazil, many times after a conversation with a friend on a tropical porch, I go home and write down some points made in our conversation and I reflect upon them" (*Politics*). Are you up for pulling a not-infrequent "all-nighter" (*Politics*) with him?

Happily, a long night lies ahead.

~~~~~~~~~~~~~~~~~~~~~~~~~~~~~~~~

AND YOUR TOPIC FOR DINNER CONVERSATION IS

"As you know, Antonio, when you live alongside other people in their everyday lives, it is a constant learning experience" (*Learning to Question*). Join the conversation between Freire and his Chilean friend and fellow exile Antonio Faundez. Tell the story of an exceptional learning experience that for you did "transcend the idea of education as pure transference of knowledge" (*Politics*). Why does this event remain powerful and memorable? Since "knowledge is not something that is made and finished" (*Politics*),

talk about things that you want to learn. Take turns naming something specific that you have learned already from each diner.

~~~~~~~~~~~~~~~~~~~~~~~~~~~~~~~~

THE DOORBELL RINGS

Guests arriving with store-bought chips and varieties of salsa can elect a twosome to mix a pitcher of *caipirinhas*, the *cachaça* (a Brazilian liquor made from sugarcane that is often referred to as Brazilian rum) and lime cocktail-of-choice for Brazil's working class. Our host Freire especially enjoyed this "national drink" on sultry summer evenings. Although locals may be conditioned to consume *caipirinhas* until the wee hours, diners may want to consider the less potent Malbec wines grown in the foothills of neighboring Argentina for a smoky, earthy complement to your evening's spicy fare. Note to host: Make sure you have a grill at-the-ready!

Bebel Gilberto names "a fruit for you," kick-starting the festivities with a taste of "Jabuticaba," singing seductively "Tanto Tempo," and, yes, it would be "So Nice" to "samba through life" with her. Bebel introduces you to her father, guitarist and vocalist João Gilberto and his saxophonist friend Stan Getz. *Getz/Gilberto* cools the evening with the pair's legendary blending of samba and jazz. Foot tapping to Brazil's bossa nova sound, listen to one or all tracks, but don't miss "Doralice" and "The Girl from Ipanema." Singing and songwriting for generations, guitarist Milton Nascimento invites you back in time to *Clube da Esquina* to meet his friend Lô Borges and "Os Povos" ("The People"), travel to "San Vicente," and to be "Tudo o Que Você Podia Ser" ("All You Can Be"). Maria Bethânia's sensitive vocal tribute to "Gente Humilde" ("Humble People") signals it's time to talk education.

The jazz Brazilian Trio thrums in the background, taking you through *Forests* and "Flying Over Rio." Enjoy their "Tarde" and "Montreux." Here he is! Welcome Brazil's perhaps most famous export, creative spark of the bossa nova style, Antonio Carlos ("Tom") Jobim. Composer and arranger, pianist and guitarist, Jobim supports the heart of your discussion with "Diálogo." Queue his tunes: "Meditation," "Insensatez" ("How Insensitive"), "Corcovado" ("Quiet Nights of Quiet Stars"), "Desafinado," "Look to the Sky," and "Mojave." Duduka Da Fonseca drums you leisurely to your feet, saying "Bye Bye Brasil" (but not really) and toasting "O Grande Amor" (most surely).

Step it up! Sergio Mendes & Brasil '66 insist you "Look Around," pointing to "So Many Stars" and such a "Mundo Hermoso" ("Pretty World"). They sing what each of us knows, that we make it through "With a Little Help from My Friends." Freire's soul mate in her criticism of the dictatorship, much-loved Elis Regina puts the finishing touch on your evening. Her duet with Tom Jobim, "Águas de Março" ("The Waters of March"), forecasts March rain that will put an end to Brazil's summer. When Regina's voice meshes with the jazz harmonica and guitar of the whistling Belgian Toots Thielemans, you'll want to sit a spell, sipping rich espresso-style *cafezinho* ("little coffee"), produced by one of a growing number of fairtrade coffee farmers in Brazil. Listen to the duo's "Canto de Ossanha," the country's theme song "Aquarela do Brasil," and take your leave with a hearty "Wave."

FISH TACOS

Starting with ingredients that Brazilians might call "barbarianly ours" ("Brazilwood," *Oxford Book of Latin American Poetry*) these recipes free foods from their traditional contexts. Indigenous ingredients used in daily fare and once relegated to second-tier status today reappear in dishes that recognize Brazil's place at the global table. Imagine the white fish in these tacos plucked from the mighty waters of the Solimões River, the Brazilian portion of the Amazon.

PREPARATION: 1 hour

3 pounds halibut, cod, or other firm white fish

⅓ cup canola oil

¼ cup plus 3 tablespoons fresh lime juice

2 jalapeño peppers, seeded and coarsely chopped, or to taste

¾ cup chopped fresh cilantro

1 jicama, peeled and cut into thin matchsticks

1 carrot, peeled and cut into thin matchsticks

3 scallions, finely chopped

2 tablespoons fish sauce

1 teaspoon sugar

¾ cup sour cream

1–2 canned chipotle chiles packed in adobo, minced

Salt, to taste

16 6-inch corn tortillas

1. Arrange the fish in a glass or other nonre-active baking dish.

2. In a small bowl, whisk together the oil, the ¼ cup of lime juice, the jalapeños, and ½ cup of the cilantro. Pour over the fish and let marinate for 25 minutes. Prepare the grill.

3. Combine the jicama, carrot, scallions, and the remaining ¼ cup cilantro in a bowl. In a separate small bowl, stir together the remaining 3 tablespoons lime juice, the fish sauce, and sugar until the sugar dis-solves completely. Pour over the jicama mixture and toss to combine.

4. In a small serving bowl, stir together the sour cream and chipotle chiles.

5. Grill the fish for 4 minutes. Turn and grill for 3 more minutes, or until nicely charred.

6. Remove the fish from the grill, salt to taste, and let rest for 5 minutes. Slice the fish into narrow strips. Heat the tortillas on the grill until just warm.

7. Have your guests fill their own tortillas with the fish and the jicama mixture and a dollop of chipotle sauce.

BLACK BEAN SALAD

Staples of Brazilian cuisine, black beans are the main ingredients in *feijoada*, a smoked-meat lunchtime favorite especially enjoyed by Freire. Tonight beans tumble about in a mix of bright colors in this spicy combination of lime, jalapeño, and tart tomatillos.

PREPARATION: 30 minutes

1 15.5-ounce can black beans, rinsed under cold water and thoroughly drained

4 tomatillos, husked and diced

2 yellow bell peppers, cored, seeded, and diced

1 avocado, peeled, pitted, and diced

½ cup diced red onion

2 teaspoons minced jalapeño pepper

1 teaspoon grated lime zest

¼ cup fresh lime juice

1 teaspoon kosher salt, or to taste

1½ teaspoons ground cumin, or to taste

¼ cup extra virgin olive oil

1. In a large serving bowl, combine the beans, tomatillos, bell peppers, avocado, onion, jalapeño, and zest.

2. In a small bowl, combine the lime juice, salt, and cumin. In a steady stream, slowly whisk in the olive oil. Pour the dressing over the bean mixture and toss to coat. Taste for seasonings, adding more salt or cumin as necessary.

COCONUT BREAD PUDDING WITH DARK RUM SAUCE

Originally concocted as a clever way to make use of stale bread, traditional bread pudding is recharged with a tropical infusion of coconut and dark rum. Evoking the native *quindim*—a sticky cake made from the palm fruit's sweet white meat—this version makes good use of Brazil's plentiful groves along northern Bahia's Coconut Coast. *Cachaça* distilleries produce fresh cane juice that fills glasses as well as fuel tanks for the country's many energy-efficient cars.

PREPARATION: 1 hour, 15 minutes (45 minutes active)

COCONUT BREAD PUDDING

1 tablespoon unsalted butter

1 loaf supermarket or other thin-crust bread (about 1 pound), slightly stale, cut or torn into 1-inch pieces

2 cups sweetened, shredded coconut

1½ cups coconut milk

2½ cups whole milk

½ cup granulated sugar

8 large eggs

1 teaspoon vanilla

½ teaspoon ground cinnamon

⅓ cup turbinado (or raw) sugar

DARK RUM SAUCE

½ cup (1 stick) unsalted butter

1 cup packed dark brown sugar

1 cup heavy cream

¼ teaspoon salt

3 tablespoons dark rum (a Caribbean, molasses-based rum yields a thicker sauce)

1. Preheat the oven to 350 degrees.

2. Butter a 9 x 13-inch baking dish with the 1 tablespoon butter. Arrange the bread pieces in the dish, sprinkle with ½ cup of the shredded coconut, and set aside.

3. In a medium saucepan, combine the coconut milk, whole milk, and granulated sugar and cook over medium heat until the sugar is dissolved. Cool slightly. Whisk the eggs briefly and stir into the milk mixture, add the vanilla and cinnamon, and then stir in 1 cup of the coconut.

4. Pour the milk mixture over the bread pieces, pressing the bread slightly to make sure that the liquid is absorbed evenly. Sprinkle with the remaining ½ cup coconut and the turbinado sugar. Bake for 45 minutes, or until golden brown and set.

5. While the bread pudding is baking, make the rum sauce. Melt the butter in a medium saucepan. Add the brown sugar and stir until dissolved. Add the cream and salt, increase heat, and cook for 1 minute. Remove from the heat and whisk in the rum. Keep warm or gently reheat before serving.

6. When you take the bread pudding from the oven, divide it into squares for individual servings and generously drizzle with the rum sauce.

BRAZIL TO GO

Read Paulo Coelho's *The Alchemist* and Clarice Lispector's *The Hour of the Star* while lying on the Cacao beaches in Bahia, and some lazy evening listen to the musical partnership of poet and bossa nova lyricist Vinicius de Moraes and guitarist Baden Powell on *Os Afros Sambas*. . . . As you are welcomed to Rio de Janeiro by a towering statue of Christ the Redeemer atop Corcovado Mountain, hit Rio's streets by watching the film *City of God*, directed by Fernando Meirelles and Kátia Lund, and visit the site of the 2014 World Cup and 2016 Summer Olympics. . . . Marvel at the collaboration between photographer Vik Muniz and the *catadores* (garbage sorters of recyclables), their stories and photographic portraits captured by Lucy Walker and Karen Harley in *Waste Land*. . . . Walk for days amidst the roaring beauty of Iguazú Falls, ride waves in Florianópolis and perhaps hit tennis balls with Gustavo ("Guga") Kuerten, have fun with street artist Bel Borba, and find *Brazilian Romance* with Sarah Vaughan. . . .

RESOURCES

PHILOSOPHY

The Politics of Education by Paulo Freire, translated by Donaldo Macedo.

Pedagogy of the Oppressed by Paulo Freire, translated by Myra Bergman Ramos.

Letters to Cristina: Reflections on My Life and Work by Paulo Freire, translated by Donaldo Macedo with Quilda Macedo and Alexandre Oliveira.

Learning to Question by Paulo Freire and Antonio Faundez, translated by Tony Coates.

MUSIC

Bebel Gilberto by Bebel Gilberto: "Jabuticaba."

Tanto Tempo by Bebel Gilberto: "Tanto Tempo," "So Nice" ("Summer Samba").

Getz/Gilberto by Stan Getz and João Gilberto: "Doralice," "The Girl from Ipanema."

Clube da Esquina by Milton Nascimento: "Os Povos" ("The People"), "San Vicente," "Tudo o Que Você Podia Ser" ("All You Can Be").

Sings the Vinicius De Moraes Songbook by Maria Bethânia: "Gente Humilde" ("Humble People").

Forests by Brazilian Trio: "Flying Over Rio," "Tarde," "Montreux."

Wave by Antonio Carlos Jobim: "Diálogo," "Look to the Sky," "Mojave."

Composer of Desafinado, Plays by Antonio Carlos Jobim: "Meditation," "Insensatez" ("How Insensitive"), "Corcovado" ("Quiet Nights of Quiet Stars"), "Desafinado."

Samba Jazz in Black and White by Duduka Da Fonseca: "Bye Bye Brasil," "O Grande Amor."

Sergio Mendes & Brasil '66—Greatest Hits: "Look Around," "So Many Stars," "Mundo Hermoso" ("Pretty World"), "With a Little Help from My Friends."

Elis & Tom by Elis Regina and Antonio Carlos Jobim: "Águas de Março" ("The Waters of March").

Aquarela do Brasil by Elis Regina and Toots Thielemans: "Canto de Ossanha," "Aquarela do Brasil," "Wave."

FOOD

The Oxford Book of Latin American Poetry: A Bilingual Anthology edited by Cecilia Vicuña and Ernesto Livon-Grosman: "Brazilwood" by Oswald de Andrade.

Rum: A Social and Sociable History of the Real Spirit of 1776 by Ian Williams.

Spiritual Hunger

JULY IN IRAQ

Diners forget napkins. Sitting on their heels, silent child philosophers slap their thighs impatiently. College students grin on the first day of class when they see the assignment on the board. Is the philosophy teacher really this fascinating? No, but the world is. The assignment: "If you could have the answer to one, just one, question, what would your question be?" Respecting the requirement of secrecy and the limitation of using just one sentence, left in solitary wonder because they must wait until the next meeting, and when the time finally arrives—fireworks in every setting! Dinner partners pat the pocket safeguarding their sentence, trying to guess who might have written the same one. College students eye classmates suspiciously. Many child philosophers, keeping perhaps their first secrets, retrieve questions stashed in hiding places. Serious philosophers clear their throats before delivering their prized questions to a hushed group, quite often repeating the questions for emphasis. The next speaker, though ready, waits and allows time for pondering. "Since everything seems to change, is anything permanent? Who decides the makings of a good life? How can I know what really matters? Can I discover perfection? Does Truth exist regardless of time and place? Why was *I* born? When will I die, what is death, and is that two questions oops or three?!"

Probing for this one question upends philosophers of all ages because the world itself amazes. What on earth (and beyond, under, and above) is going on? Really going on . . . was going on . . . will go on, and on. . . . Awe comes easily. Feel it: Zapped into a cosmos that stretches with every question I ask and with every new thing I learn, I am blown away by, and thrust into, the world's grandeur. I wonder. What about consciousness? What *is* it? What has it, what doesn't, or does consciousness saturate everything? Are time and infinity *both* real? How accurately do my senses relay the world to me? What else is out there that I'm missing? What lies within me, untapped? (Me?) If certain knowledge is possible, how would we *know* when we knew? Do other beings exist whose capacity for experiencing the world takes them closer to reality? Contemplating the breadth of the Arabian Desert, the one-day flight of the mayfly, the whale's song, the hardening of the baby porcupine's quills, and the mourning of the dead shared by members of an elephant herd. . . .

Zeroing in on the resemblances and repetition in the natural world, I'm struck by a sense of order. Look! Likeness appears in the human hand and the sand crab, the uncoiling layers of a fern, the whiskers on catfish and cat and Carl. Staring at a wintry pond, all the "different" ice cracks splinter in an identical pattern. A dive underwater reveals self-similarity in the mustard sea fan and the branching fire coral attached to it. Leaning on a fence, my eye catches the lichen's intricate design and the moss on a nearby statue that gives the rider on horseback a neatly trimmed beard. How did all this happen? Design or fluke, with or without purpose, the world exists. Why? Wasn't the existence of absolutely nothing an alternative? Egad! What could nothing *be*? Awe, and then some.

Asking the burning questions brings

both excitement and consolation to philosophy circles. "When people ask the same question it makes us closer." "Mystery charms us if we let it and I'd rather live with it than without it." "I've never talked about what I would like to know, much less all the things that I *know* I never will. Cheers for not putting a lid on it." Striving for the Truth about it All feels packaged into our humanity. Oh for the sweet satisfaction of knowing *that* one reality, the knowledge of which makes everything else more than okay. Understanding even one thing through and through, absorbing the essence of something that never changes, knowing *why*—what contentment such comprehension would bring. Perfection.

Awe inspires this spiritual hunger, the desire to blow past human limitations and reach beyond our ordinary ways of knowing. The spiritual quest springs alive in the innermost part of our being, sparking an urge for an understanding that transcends rational knowledge. The spirit aches for intimate contact with the Whole, an inborn drive to touch the intangible. Conversing late into the evening, an awestruck philosopher described his greatest wish: "I long for resonance with everything, so completely integrated into the world that all my questions disappear. Imagine." A child philosopher begs me to "stop saying 'good question' and give us the right answer about why life is." Why life? Sorry, kids. Appetites whetted for another kind of food, diners repeatedly express their appreciation for the chance to wander into the unknown together. At ease and loosening up by the minute, they willingly put aside personal convictions in order to enrich their group exploration.

Here's how it feels to me. Come to the beach. Sifting sand between our fingers, we gaze ever-outward at the ocean, far out and eyes straining. Yes, a line appears where sea and sky meet. This tantalizing end point doesn't look unreachable, so we climb into our little dinghy and row toward the horizon. Getting closer! Oars splashing! Vastness expands and surrounds us as we push on. Hah, didn't expect this. Rowing, rowing, the world is bigger than we thought. That elusive line backtracks yet pulls us magnetically forward. Paddling stops. Now no line separates sky and water—if it ever did. Everything spreads its arms, no boundaries. Thrilling, humbling, provocative, and magnificent. Tired and speechless we head for shore, aware that our rowing will continue with every tomorrow, the search irresistible. Minnow and pelican whisper that something huge is going on, and being part of it makes us want to know the world through and through. Our rowing expedition serves as symbol for the universal hunger of the spirit to hold the Truth in human hands. Bring IT on.

With the wind at our backs, our rowboat takes us into the Persian Gulf. Coming ashore, we head for eleventh-century Baghdad to find a university law professor who is starving spiritually and emotionally. Abu Hamid Muhammad al-Ghazali sought certainty and found it after a long, tortuous struggle. In an immediate flash of insight, he experienced Truth as Allah, as God. We set off with al-Ghazali on his treasure hunt. Each of us tracks fresh footprints in the sand, making the search for inner completion our own. Finders keepers.

PREPPING FOR IRAQ

Listen to the *Maqams of Baghdad*, performed by the Safaafir Iraqi Maqam Ensemble, walk along the Tigris bridge in Mosul, learn about journalist Atwar Bahjat's last visit to Samarra as you stroll around the mosque at Al-Askari, and marvel at the ancient ruins surrounding the Great Ziggurat of Ur, with a stop in nearby Nasiriyah. . . . View the stunning body art of Wafaa Bilal and Sama Alshaibi and the flamboyant architecture of Pritzker Prize–winner Zaha Hadid. . . . Tune into Al Jazeera's English version of Arabic news, and watch the powerful documentaries *Control Room*, directed by Jehane Noujaim, and David Fine's *Salaam Dunk.* . . . Meet the women in Heather Raffo's *9 Parts of Desire*, reading the play and catching a live performance, if possible, and examine Geraldine Brooks's book *Nine Parts of Desire: The Hidden World of Islamic Women*. . . . Review a map of ancient Persia and pinpoint al-Ghazali's hometown, Tus, an area in present-day Iran. . . .

liverance from Error, he insists that if you want to know for sure, you must be willing to toss aside anything that contains the tiniest seed of doubt. After more than ten years devoted to his investigation, al-Ghazali experienced the peace that comes with certainty through the way laid out by Sufi mystics.

Where will you find your place to rest? Start your engines. Prepare for liftoff.

IMMEDIATE EXPERIENCE IS LIKE
ACTUALLY WITNESSING A THING
AND TAKING IT IN ONE'S HAND.

AL-GHAZALI,
Deliverance from Error

Seekers of all backgrounds find a friend in al-Ghazali. They relate to his skepticism about both the reliability of our senses and the certainty assumed in mathematics and science. In his spiritual autobiography, *De-*

SEARCHING

"As I drew near the age of adolescence the bonds of mere authority ceased to hold me and inherited beliefs lost their grip . . ." (*Deliverance*). Secure in his prestigious position as visiting professor of law at the University of Baghdad, al-Ghazali's youthful inquisitiveness still tugged hard. Feeling trapped by material preoccupations and the demands of public life, a reputable teacher of theology yet dissatisfied in his soul, he determined to find certainty. He examined the two sources of his current knowledge with relentless precision. Was there any reason to doubt the testimony of his senses? Could he count on the first principles taken for granted as the underpinning of mathematics? If even one qualm surfaced, then he must dismiss that source of knowledge and look elsewhere for certainty. Let's go where he goes.

"From where does this reliance on sense perception come? The most powerful sense is the sense of sight" (*Deliverance*), so al-Ghazali pokes here first. How can we be sure that what we see is a faithful copy of reality? Very few twenty-first-century philosophers wait for al-Ghazali's field report. Giggling children whip off eyeglasses and vividly describe their altered views of the world. The teacher looks fuzzy, of course, and they can't read their homework assignments or decipher the signs on bathroom doors. Chaos in the classroom: "Which is the real world, the one I see with or without my glasses?" Perplexed college students find it impossible to discover whether or not we all see the same color on the book jacket: "How can we talk about 'green'? Maybe we're all color-blind!" Diners step outside and watch the sun go down, agreeing with al-Ghazali's assessment that everyone "looks at the heavenly body (sun) and sees it as small, the size of a shilling; yet geometric computations show that it is greater than the size of the earth" (*Deliverance*).

Rather than being alarmed, al-Ghazali's fellow skeptics delight in uncertainty's many faces. Food becomes funny when no two descriptions of a sauce are alike. Can one dish be salty, sweet, hot, bland, *and* tart all at once? What is it, really? Last night's concertgoers now debate whether they listened to the same music. How can they know that they heard the same tones and range of instruments? Why did some people leave at intermission and others clap for an encore? The temperature of the classroom is too warm for some, too cool for others. Is one room really both hot *and* cold? Of this we and al-Ghazali are sure: "I could no longer trust sense perception" (*Deliverance*). One source of knowledge falls way short of certainty.

But "I know that ten is more than three" (*Deliverance*), al-Ghazali assures us. Even if our senses prove unreliable, we can trust basic "intellectual principles," such as "the same thing cannot be affirmed and denied" (*Deliverance*). Or can we? Once again, amused doubters follow his lead. Math students of every age and level admit that "math is the game we play, but there could be other games with completely different rules." Science students tick off repeated instances when one discovery after another yielded unfolding layers of the unknown, "from Galileo to Einstein to Feynman to the Higgs boson particle." Far from resurrecting the assumptions that lay the foundation of math and science, al-Ghazali removes all answers from the back of the book with this question: "Why are you confident that all

your waking beliefs, whether from sense or intellect, are real" (*Deliverance*)? When we awaken, don't we recognize our dreams as illusions, regardless of how powerful and believable they seemed during the night? Yes? Hold on tight. Capitalizing on our hesitation, the Baghdad scholar finishes his dance with doubt, teasing us that "perhaps life in this world is a dream" (*Deliverance*). How can we know that it's not? Yipes.

There's no turning back or away now. Shaken awake, al-Ghazali's hunters prepare for anything. Rooting out so much uncertainty invigorates rather than discourages. With our minds cleansed and our spirits lifted, the way clears. Now we have a chance to experience what *is*. No doubt about it.

SATISFIED

Al-Ghazali exhausted the sources of knowledge that were easily available to him. If certainty evaded him via sensory and intellectual routes, was there no end to his "unhealthy condition" (*Deliverance*)? Detaching himself from family, colleagues, job, and city life, he basked in purifying desert solitude. This journey, inspired by Sufi mysticism, prepared him for something more certain than knowledge. What could be more certain than knowledge? Al-Ghazali entered the indescribable state of union of the human with the divine. His spirit free at last, separation evaporated between the seeker and the sought, between al-Ghazali and Allah. Spirit is spirit. This "complete absorption in God . . . is hard to describe in language" (*Deliverance*). Book smarts are no substitute for "tasting" (*Deliverance*) the Truth. After knocking at the door of knowledge, trying to force his way inside using reason and language, he burst through these barriers into another realm. The door behind which certainty had been hiding disappeared, the unthinkable experience of the Unknown unveiled.

Ah! The Unknown can be the Experienced. Study, thought, and seeking fade into the peace of union. Words fail, any "proof" of this inner eyewitness experience is impossible. It is IT. "What a difference between *knowing* the definition of health . . . and *being* healthy . . . the definition of drunkenness and *being* drunk" (*Deliverance*). Those who travel with al-Ghazali smile as his yearning ceases, identifying with his soul satisfaction in various ways. His realization that experience alone holds the key to fulfillment triggers memories of union with Life. Appreciating that his certainty came through his personal experience of Allah, my partners in philosophy find much in common with the Muslim scholar. They effortlessly transfer into their own lives his original spiritual hunger and its eventual satisfaction.

How I've wished that al-Ghazali could eavesdrop on the ways in which his discovery of the Truth dovetails with seekers and finders in a very different century. Diners' words hit a wall, but carefully chosen, they point the way. A runner speaks about the joyful absorption in life found in the repetitive slap, slap, slap of shoe on earth, a rhythm matched by her heart's beat, beat, beat. A drummer experiences this same joining, hands rapping on drum skin, bare feet tapping on solid earth, space and sound, rat-a-tat-tat. An unexpected touch of empathy exposes Life at its core to the recipient immersed in grief, soup warming on his stove somehow explaining everything. Nature provides the avenue to union for hiking, swimming, and gardening philosophers— climber merges with mountain trail, swimmer's kicking legs join with water, and gardener's caked knees wear dirt. Those engaged in and by the creative process likewise experience peaks of fulfillment. A writer describes his craft as a process of hanging all his words on a coat rack until he suddenly knows exactly what to "wear." An artist applies paint to canvas with such intensity that she forgets that I (and she) am there. A guitarist scribbles notes to match his words and one song comes alive. A despairing doctor, taken aback by an act of generosity that the giver could ill afford financially, finds her connection with Life restored. "Beyond the intellect there is yet another stage. In this another eye is opened, by which he beholds the unseen" (*Deliverance*). *This* seeing is believing.

Children thrive whenever they "talk about the same thing as the philosopher but in different ways." Big intuition is spoken in little voices. "Deep laughing takes me there," a child explains after walking al-Ghazali's path. "You have to be a certain way for a laugh to make itself. Laughter tells me everything I need to know." Adults stare off in the distance as this simple statement rings true. The child philosopher adds for clarification, "I think it's perfect because I forget myself when I laugh." Young philosophers relate to al-Ghazali's alone time in the desert. "When I am by myself and my mind roams, no plans, I sink into myself and things become still. I'm floating and I'm everything." More stares from the grown-ups. "What about love no matter what?" a fourth grader asks. "Isn't that about All?" Is it, after all?

Our imperfect selves grind on toward fulfillment. Al-Ghazali returned to his teaching and we go back to our lives. We trust, as he trusts, in what our senses capture and in the worthiness of those multiplication tables . . . mostly. So what if our desire to complete ourselves meets with frustration. Those "other things which are beyond the ken of the intellect" (*Deliverance*) turn us on, really turn us "on." Enrolled in his first philosophy course and grappling with al-Ghazali, an engineering major sighed, "This odd, empty feeling that I can't get it all fills me up."

Those who dine on philosophy know. Hungry when they arrive, sharing fine food aplenty well into the night, they leave starving. Perfectly satisfying.

AND YOUR TOPIC FOR DINNER CONVERSATION IS

"To thirst after a comprehension of things as they really are was my habit and custom from a very early age. It was instinctive to me, a part of my God-given nature, a matter of temperament and not of my choice or contriving" (*Deliverance*). Do you share al-Ghazali's "thirst"? How *are* things, *really*? What would you like to know beyond a doubt? Are your senses trustworthy? How about math and science? What else? Talk Truth.

THE DOORBELL RINGS

Against the backdrop of extravagant banquets enjoyed by the Islamic rulership in Baghdad at the time, al-Ghazali cautioned that food was a "distasteful necessity" (*al-Ghazali's Book of Fear and Hope*). In keeping with this assessment, guests should seek unpretentious yet delicious contributions to the evening. Hummus, a creamy chick pea spread, is widely available and also very easy to make from scratch. The Arabic expression "there is bread and salt between us" (*Day of Honey: A Memoir of Food, Love, and War*) reminds us that disagreements disappear after sharing food, and any Middle Eastern meal without flatbreads (pita or naan, for example) would be incomplete. Some diners may want to brave a few sips of *arak*, a potent, milky-white alcoholic beverage sold in Middle Eastern specialty shops, while others can contribute beer in honor of its Mesopotamian origins that stretch back six thousand years. Top off the evening with a dessert of candied fruit or crystallized citrus peels.

The meditative repetition of percussion and *oud* (an unfretted, wide-necked lute, plucked with a *risha*, featured in Arabic music) heard in Sufi mosques captivated Saadoun Al-Bayati, and his *Songs of Iraq* welcome you to his native land. His "Iraqi 6" inspires some hip shaking, and fellow *oud* player and child of Baghdad Rahim Alhaj appears *When the Soul Is Settled*. Alhaj blends modern improvisation with traditional Iraqi musical scales in "Taqsim Maqam Saba" and "Taqsim Maqam Kurd." Flow down *Two Rivers* with jazz trumpeter, composer, vocalist, and *santoor*-player (seventy-stringed hammered dulcimer) Amir ElSaffar. What a smooth glide into the evening discussion, listening to his "The Blues in E Half-Flat," a gentle "Flood," and "Awj Intro."

Khyam Allami meshes *Resonance/Dissonance*, Iraq/England, and traditional/contemporary. Sink with him into "Reverie" and "Individuation" complemented by "Tawazon I: Balance." Feel the "Trance" evoked by peace activist Yair Dalal and the Al Ol Ensemble. Arab and Israeli influences mix with *oud* and violin in Dalal's "Silan" and "Min Hamidbar." Internationally celebrated Ahmed Mukhtar showcases music's crucial role in the Sufi tradition in his *Rhythms of Baghdad*. Know al-Ghazali's world even better as Mukhtar serves a buffet of treats to take your conversation to a satisfying conclusion: Sway to the *riqq* (tambourine) in "Fingers and Sambales," catch "Sufi Rhythm" in the *tar* (long, double-bowl-shaped lute) solo, and twitch your shoulders to the beat of the *khishba* (small drum hanging by a cord from the musician's shoulder) in "Kasor."

Stay awhile. Steep black tea with a crushed cardamom pod and serve in small, Middle Eastern–style heatproof glasses accompanied by lumps of sugar. Vocalist and guitarist Ilham Al Madfai bids "Farewell to the Sands" and offers his prayer "Allah Alayek" ("God Be With You"). Famed *oud* maestro Munir Bashir pays your ticket "From Baghdad to Granada" and gets your heels clicking to the "Rock of the Oud." Iraqi poet and peace ambassador Kadim Al Sahir joins his voice with Sarah Brightman's in his composition "The War Is Over Now." *Salām*. Peace.

In the Kitchen

MEDJOOL DATES WITH CHEESE AND HONEY

With the classic introduction "There was one, and there wasn't one" (*The Greenwood Encyclopedia of Folktales and Fairy Tales*), ancient Persian fairy tales tempt young (and older) minds into a state of suspended belief. Like our own once-upon-a-time stories that expect the unexpected, these narratives draw listeners into an uncertain world. Medjool dates, stuffed with creamy mascarpone and sprinkled with salt and honey, mingle salty and sweet flavors and test each diner's differing perceptions. As you sink your teeth into the flesh of these dried fruits, consider whether the taste is sweet or salty or something altogether different. . . .

PREPARATION: 30 minutes

24 Medjool, or other large dates

6 tablespoons mascarpone cheese, at room temperature

2 tablespoons plain Greek-style yogurt

Extra virgin olive oil, for drizzling

Honey, for drizzling

Fleur de sel, or other coarse-grained sea salt, for sprinkling

1. Preheat the oven to 400 degrees.

2. With a sharp knife, make a lengthwise slit partway through each date and carefully remove the pit to create a pocket.

3. In a small bowl, blend the mascarpone and yogurt to make the filling. Insert 1 teaspoon of the filling into each date.

4. Place the stuffed dates on a baking sheet. Bake for 5 minutes, or until the filling softens. Do not overcook or the filling will become runny.

5. Drizzle with olive oil and several drops of honey and sprinkle with fleur de sel. Serve warm.

EGGPLANT TWO WAYS

Artists working in the flourishing new capital city of Baghdad were known for their miniature illustrations of mystical motifs and lush gardens. Thinking the use of perspective an optical ruse that impeded enlightenment, painters in search of divine experience layered flattened scenes to be viewed from multiple positions. Practice the art of shifting perspective by preparing eggplant, a versatile fixture in the Middle Eastern diet for centuries, two ways. Who would know, at first glance, that the eggplant's glossy, rich-hued surface conceals a soft, meaty interior? Sprinkle your eggplant dishes with pomegranate seeds, the gem-like treasures hidden inside fruits harvested from ancient Persia's tree of knowledge.

EGGPLANT ONE WAY

PREPARATION: 1 hour, 15 minutes (30 minutes active)

3–4 medium-sized eggplants (less than 1 pound each)

3 tablespoons tahini (sesame paste)

3 cloves garlic, peeled and minced

3 tablespoons fresh lemon juice

3 tablespoons extra virgin olive oil

½ teaspoon ground cumin

1 teaspoon kosher salt

Toasted wedges of flatbread, naan, or pita, for serving

1. Prepare an outdoor grill. (Or preheat oven to 400 degrees.)

2. Using a fork, pierce the eggplants all over. Grill the eggplants until softened and collapsed, about 30 minutes. (Or, roast the eggplants on a baking sheet for 20 minutes until soft, then broil for 10 more minutes, until they begin to char.) Allow the eggplants to cool.

3. Cut the stems off the tops of the eggplants and cut each eggplant in half lengthwise. Using a spoon, scrape the pulp from the eggplant skins into a colander. Discard the skins and allow the pulp to drain in the sink for 10 minutes.

4. Mash by hand (or combine in a food processor), the eggplant pulp, tahini, garlic, lemon juice, olive oil, cumin, and salt.

5. Transfer to a bowl and serve with toasted wedges of flatbread, naan, or pita.

EGGPLANT ANOTHER WAY

PREPARATION: 1 hour

4 medium eggplants (2–3 inches in diameter), sliced into ½-inch-thick slices

¼ cup plus 1 tablespoon extra virgin olive oil

1 clove garlic, peeled and minced

¼ cup honey

½ cup buttermilk

½ cup plain Greek-style yogurt

1 tablespoon pomegranate molasses (available at Middle Eastern specialty shops)[1]

¼ teaspoon cayenne pepper

¼ teaspoon kosher salt

½ cup walnuts, coarsely chopped

---

1. Pomegranate molasses can be made by combining 4 cups of pomegranate juice, ½ cup sugar, and ¼ cup fresh lemon juice and cooking over medium-high heat until the sugar is completely dissolved. Reduce the heat to low and simmer for approximately 1 hour, until thickened. Cool before using. The extra pomegranate molasses will keep in the refrigerator for several weeks.

1 pomegranate

3 cups uncooked couscous, prepared according to package instructions

1. Preheat the oven to 400 degrees.

2. Toss the eggplant slices in a bowl with the ¼ cup olive oil, the garlic, and honey. Arrange the eggplant slices in one layer on baking sheets and cook for 25 minutes, or until nicely browned. Turn the eggplant slices and continue to cook on the other side for 10 minutes, or until browned.

3. While the eggplant is cooking, combine the buttermilk, yogurt, the 1 tablespoon olive oil, the pomegranate molasses, cayenne, and salt. Chill until needed.

4. Heat the walnuts in a dry skillet over medium-low heat until fragrant, 5–10 minutes. Stir frequently.

5. Using a small knife, cut off the pomegranate's crown and make 4 cuts from stem to stem in the rind. Submerge the pomegranate in a bowl of water (to avoid staining your hands and the work surface) and gently pull its rind apart and peel away the white, papery skin to expose the seeds. The seeds will sink to the bottom of the bowl. Transfer the seeds to a small bowl and reserve for garnishing.

6. Arrange the couscous in a mound on a platter. Top with the eggplant slices and generously drizzle with the buttermilk sauce. Sprinkle with the walnuts and garnish with the desired amount of pomegranate seeds.

IRAQ TO GO

Rock in the "cradle of civilization," Meso-potamia, tracing the courses of the Tigris and Euphrates Rivers and appreciating the culture of ancient Sumerians, and learn about engineer Azzam Alwash's plans to restore Mesopotamian wetlands in David Johnson's episode on *Nature*: "Braving Iraq". . . . Study the Baghdad Renaissance Plan, detailed by architect Hisham Ashk-ouri, and applaud The Organization of Women's Freedom in Iraq, founded by Yanar Mohammed. . . . Cheer on soccer striker Younis Mahmoud Khalaf and sprinter Dana Hussein Abdul-Razzaq. . . . See the country from within as subjects film them-selves in Yasmine Hanani's documentary *Voices of Iraq*, backed by the hip-hop group Euphrates. . . . Find out more about Raed Jarrar's blog and his T-shirt, and dial in women's Radio Al-Mahaba. . . . Imagine with Sufi poetess Bibi Hayati "Before there was a trace of this world of men," listen to Rida Al Abdullah's protest song "Wein-kom Ya Arab," and research the musical legacies of *maqam* songstress Farida and Iraqi/Jewish brothers Doud and Saleh Al-Kuwaity. . . .

RESOURCES

PHILOSOPHY

"Deliverance from Error," Abu Hamid Muhammad al-Ghazali, in *The Faith and Practice of al-Ghazali*, translated by W. Montgomery Watt.

MUSIC

Songs of Iraq by Saadoun Al-Bayati: "Iraqi 6."

When the Soul Is Settled: Music of Iraq by Rahim Alhaj: "Taqsim Maqam Saba," "Taqsim Maqam Kurd."

Two Rivers by Amir ElSaffar: "The Blues in E Half-Flat," "Flood," "Awj Intro."

Resonance/Dissonance by Khyam Allami: "Reverie," "Individuation," "Tawazon I: Balance."

Silan by Yair Dalal and the Al Ol Ensemble: "Trance," "Silan," "Min Hamidbar."

Rhythms of Baghdad by Ahmed Mukhtar: "Fingers and Sambales," "Sufi Rhythm," "Kasor."

Khuttar by Ilham Al Madfai: "Farewell to the Sands."

The Voice of Iraq by Ilham Al Madfai: "Allah Alayek" ("God Be with You").

Rhythm & Melodies by Munir Bashir: "From Baghdad to Granada," "Rock of the Oud."

Harem by Sarah Brightman: "The War Is Over Now" with Kadim Al Sahir.

FOOD

al-Ghazali's Book of Fear and Hope by Abu Hamid Muhammad al-Ghazali, translated by William McKane.

Day of Honey: A Memoir of Food, Love, and War by Annia Ciezadlo.

The Greenwood Encyclopedia of Folktales and Fairy Tales by Donald Haase.

"Depiction of Wine in Persian Miniature" by Reza Sarhangi. pages.towson.edu

Plenty: Vibrant Recipes from London's Ottolenghi by Yotam Ottolenghi.

What About Love?

AUGUST IN KENTUCKY

Goofiness overtakes philosophy circles. Children giggle, point fingers, and hide faces behind see-through hands. College students skip the first class discussion, returning only when classmates give them the "all clear!" Diners' customary bonhomie temporarily evaporates. Feet shuffle and tap, legs cross and uncross, low whispers contrast with loud pronouncements, and awkward laughter accompanies quickly averted eyes. Since when does "I know it when I see it" satisfy philosophical inquiry? Sometimes a quote from a favorite author substitutes for one's own answer. Pleading voices beg "just look it up in the dictionary." Smart people try at best "not to say something stupid." Talkative philosophers discover silence. Sure enough, when the conversation turns to an examination of love, the first response is fear and flight.

Every prospect excited me as I chose the topics for this book, especially an exploration of love. But secretly I thought, *uh oh*. I know too well the challenge of writing simply and invitingly about a concept that, although so vital to our welfare, regrettably lies smothered by fluff and confusion. How to ensure that diners won't shy away from their discussion? "You'll be fine, nobody knows what love is," a friend (sort of) encouraged me. Then out of nowhere, the memory of this event tickled me without reservation on my writing way. After visiting a fourth-grade class on Valentine's Day and seeing the children off, the teacher and I chatted while clearing desks. Laughing wildly she waved a scribbled note carelessly abandoned by its recipient: "I love you. Don't be cheating on me. (P.S. What's your name anyway?)"

Laughing at all the misconceptions restores comfort and revives eagerness for a good talk about love. Initial embarrassment disappears as thinkers first dismiss unrealistic cultural stereotypes of romantic love. What a relief, I hear, to toss aside the off-putting association of love with the fairy tale sold in advertising, film and song, greeting cards and holiday set-ups. Most often I then encourage a survey of love outside the human realm for an effortless conversational jumpstart. No one ever becomes self-conscious when thinking of philosophy as the *love* of wisdom! Talk of love comes free

and easy. Love for the river whose reliable rocking has been a steady presence since childhood. Love of gardening and cooking the harvest, the fulfillment of planted seed served as nourishing vegetable. Love for the animal that erases any reticence to show affection. Music lovers abound, testifying to love's connective power, while sports lovers hook listeners with descriptions of teamwork, dirty uniforms, and that gym smell. Everyone relates, naming their own beloved spots in nature or detailing treasured pieces of music. We realize together that our loves have this in common—we love the river or the sport just as it is, as well as for what it brings to us. Sure of love so far, we now track love's presence into human interactions.

What *is* love? Clarity quickens while we search, as if for the first time, for the essence of a worn-out word. Join one especially animated dinner group as members creep closer to love. What a night! First, battling cobwebs, we go around the table taking one-word stabs at a definition. Love is: acceptance, energy, pouring, nonjudgment, willingness, creation, bonding, color. Settling in, diners write out more complete answers, scratch through lines and start over, and put pencils down and get ready to take their turn. "Love is, in fact, patient and kind, neither manufactured nor bought. It lifts you when you surrender to it. That's it. Love is happy subordination to something larger than me." One hard-won answer inspires another. "Only love gives purpose. It is emotional warmth kindled by connection and knowledge, understanding and being understood, mutual growth of spirit." Bread breaks. "Love is commitment to someone or something, a child or an idea, a commitment that demands that we preserve and protect it. The need to experience love seems to be hardwired in whether we like it or not. Like the weed growing in a cement driveway, it finds a way." Nodding in appreciation, Beryl's companion suggests his somewhat differing response: "Love isn't an idea. It's an experience of gratitude when totally exposed to another person, being just fine when naked to the bone." Beverage splashing stops and diners sink into private reflection. Then a question suggests the daunting necessity for an investigation of self-love: "Could you or I experience that same gratitude for exposure, for nakedness, when looking in the mirror?"

Why the dull ache of negativity surrounding self-love? Child philosophers claim that they feel bad about themselves. College students, sure that they don't measure up, blanket themselves in thick layers of guilt and blame. Many diners are shocked that they never thought about loving themselves until this conversation. Reality strikes when the importance of self-love becomes obvious. "If I don't love myself, I can't love my life or anybody. Can't give what you don't have." "It's so peculiar to think that I wouldn't love the person closest to me who I spend all my time with. Have I divorced myself?" "Got to make myself somebody I love because I'm stuck with me!"

For a perfect example of the merger of self-love, love of living, and love of others, I present a bright, personable high school junior, a talented singer and songwriter. Danny loves life, especially mashed potatoes and cross-country, banana pancakes and sandals—and an expansive circle of family, friends, classmates, and teachers reciprocate his magnetic love. Suddenly, troubling symptoms find him and his father, Frank, in a physician's office hearing test results that lay bare Danny's terminal diagnosis. As they listen with incredulity, the boy asks his dad, "How are you doing, Poppy?" Danny invited Frank and all who knew him from that moment on to "follow my lead," determined to live to the max, with those he loved living fully, as well. Danny kept on loving into his second year of college, elevating spirits in hospital rooms with his guitar and laugh, studying for tests and cruising with pals. He asked to be remembered only for "my loves . . . all those I loved and loved me." One foundation in his memory at his alma mater assists college students who are coping with disabling illness in continuing their class work. Another organization brings music to children and young adults undergoing cancer treatment. Love still follows Danny's lead.

Hustling into the kitchen, bell hooks announces, based on her own experience, "that much of what we were taught about the nature of love makes no sense when applied to daily life" (*All About Love*). Huddled around the counter, we follow her love recipe from scratch, learning "to mix various ingredients—care, affection, recognition, respect, commitment, and trust as well as open and honest communication" (*All About Love*).

PREPPING FOR KENTUCKY

Trek the Red River Gorge canyons, applaud members of the Kentucky Music Hall of

Fame, read any(every!)thing by Lanes Landing farming philosopher Wendell Berry, and pick a tune by Ricky Skaggs, Patty Loveless, and Tom T. Hall. . . . Enter Louisville along Muhammad Ali Boulevard, its namesake voted Kentucky's athlete of the century, take in a show during the Humana Festival of New American Plays at the Actors Theatre on Main Street, and catch a performance by the renowned Louisville Orchestra. . . . Swing a Louisville Slugger as you roam the factory, and before leaving the city take a peek into the church gym where My Morning Jacket records "Circuital," in "the same place we started out. . . ." Visit "Paradise" with Dwight Yoakam's vocal tribute to famed guitar-picker Merle Travis's Muhlenberg County hometown, and then travel back "down to Green River," as Yoakam sings, for camping at Turnhole Bend and exploring the world's longest known maze in Mammoth Cave National Park. . . .

LOVE IS AN ACTION, A PARTICIPATORY EMOTION.

BELL HOOKS,
All About Love

Gloria Jean Watkins grew up in the small, segregated town of Hopkinsville, Kentucky. Adopting the name (in lower case) of her great-grandmother "bell hooks," she pens books of social criticism and self-discovery, one work devoted to an unsentimental "philosophical undertaking" titled *All About Love*. Starting out with the definition that "it is an action we take on behalf of our own or another's spiritual growth" (*All About Love*), she acknowledges her past mistakes and misunderstandings that fueled her determination to know love. Throw back the covers, shower in cold water, and roll up your sleeves. It's time to clean house. Now we'll dance a slow Kentucky two-step: Step, and love your whole self . . . and, step, and love others, wholly.

INSIDE

The dance of love begins, and step one. . . .

Though self-love grounds love of all kinds, its reputation suffers from charges of arrogance and selfishness. Self-love is the wise and indeed only choice, however, for those who long to "shape our destinies in ways that maximize our well-being . . . valuing and nurturing human life" (*All About Love*). The willful decision to establish an honest relationship with myself, to accept and to get to know better this person, lays love's foundation. Internalizing hook's ingredients of respect, commitment, and trust, I nourish my humanity while setting the table for loving others. This work of love must begin at home, where a nitpicky housecleaning will eventually uncover love for the homebody. Each of us opens our own front door, waving philosopher hooks inside, trash bins and scrub brushes at the ready.

What a wreck! Just a glance reveals accumulations of junk bought in love's name. I'm stumbling over piles of cynicism, stacks of cultural tapes playing what love should be, and boxes of withering self-criticism. Here lurk the costly purchases that depleted my self-esteem. Going room by room, I'll collect this bag of tricks and buy back my sense of self-worth.

Door #1: Cynicism. Since it's less trouble to whine about love's absence than it is to seek the reality, I've made fun of its possibility, celebrating every disappointment. I jump to point out its failures in my life and in yours, in fiction and in "reality shows." It was in her childhood that hooks first sowed cynicism's seeds, when love was "always and only about good feeling, something given" (*All About Love*) rather than demonstrated in action. She toughened her sore heart and built defenses against teenage put-downs and adult domination. Fellow diners/cleaners recall similar demands to do better, be more, and think a certain way, all of which deflated individual personalities. Never stopping to define love and thereby risk vulnerability, they describe their expertise in masking emotions and wielding sarcasm. Some wary soul-searchers confide, as hooks does, that "the panic to find a partner was easier to manage than thinking about love" (*All About Love*). Housecleaning Solutions: Constructively revisit the past. X-ray and treat old hurt. Don't wallow. Move on. Cynicism shows itself, a self-indulgent cop-out.

Door #2: Social cues. Like hooks, I've been suspicious of these looping "negative voices" (*All About Love*), petty thieves of my individuality. Rub out the robbers' stains with these Housecleaning Solutions: Cancel my subscription to that magazine painting an impossible picture of how I should look, where I should live, and whose arm should be woven around my itty-bitty waist. Off

goes the commercial that glamorizes the perfect family that is nothing that I could or would want. No more humming along with lyrics that I pray don't come true. Not only will I quit looking for a person like me in the movies, I'm going to look for a person just like me in the mirror. Why did it take so long to realize that "in popular culture love is always the stuff of fantasy" (*All About Love*)?

Door #3: Criticism. I'm recycling myself in old patterns of harsh, be(and me)littling judgment about me first and you next. My parents tried to please their parents with my life at the same time that teachers lamented my wasted potential. Expecting criticism, I heap it on myself even when others praise me. I read high school reunion news, always the sorriest of the bunch. I set myself up for and ensure tailspins—my colleagues won't include me, my family won't call, my accent, clothes, and manners betray me. And, of course, everything about you irks me like crazy. Fuming in this gross self-image, I multiply my problems. Even when outwardly successful, my inner emptiness bubbles. I manufacture drama, "acting out" (*All About Love*) in uncontrolled, destructive, and short-lived emotional release. I do myself in and I do myself without. Housecleaning Solutions: Recognize the old ways and stop defeating my life. Drop my "act," and now act positively: Go easy on me, and you. Forgive me, and you. Treat me like someone I love, and you. Openly be me while you be you. Confident that I'm worth a life, I respect yours. Aware and on the offensive against old mistakes, I gradually slip into my skin and soul.

Yes, "it is no easy task to be self-loving" (*All About Love*), but the alternatives ate up my life. Admiring my clean house, finally I can bid low self-esteem farewell. No longer broke, I give myself some credit. Ready for step two, I step. . . .

OUTSIDE

Self-acceptance fills me with determination to support the growth of my whole self. I'll carve my identity from my strengths and shortcomings, maximize my sense of well-being with ongoing home improvement, and cultivate a watchful eye for recurring clutter. I'm learning to feed myself, storing nutrition by reading a book in a sunny nook, preparing an omelet, skateboarding, bird-watching, writing a letter, painting the fence, playing with kids, looking at photographs, or swimming after a chess match. My sense of self withstands setbacks when they come. Self-love supplies a sturdy springboard for extending this most basic love into the world. Love's definition of nourishing my and another's spiritual growth stays alive within me, and I develop new appreciation for solitude and friendship.

"Knowing how to be solitary is central. When we can be alone, we can be with others without using them as means of escape. Loneliness is painful; solitude is peaceful" (*All About Love*). With a spirited inner life, I'm invigorated when ensconced in solitude. Being with me deepens my self-awareness. Diners salute alone time: "I avoided it completely when I was on the run. Now I seek its power." "If I'm quiet, by myself, things sort themselves out." "If I enjoy my company, so will you." Promising themselves solitude, "every day some," "some nights all," a day when necessary "to reconnoiter with myself," hardworking philosophers cherish this oldest/newest gift.

Five loving faces advertise friendship's reward at an annual women's weekend retreat, laughing in agreement when their table is labeled a "love fest," touting one another's virtues and teaching other attendees all about love. Thrown off course when romantic love looms as the pinnacle of all achievement, we demote friends to secondary considerations, shorting bonds that deserve loving attention. "Often we take friendships for granted even when they are the interactions where we experience mutual pleasure" (*All About Love*), and hooks reminds us of the high standards set between friends, a rigor that we would do well to apply to all relationships. Dinner companions agree that "we trust that our friend desires our good" (*All About Love*) and we are unafraid to speak up when that trust feels threatened. But in puzzling contrast: "I'm timid with my wife." "I let my father make fun of me." "My boyfriend gets away with ridicule." Since all loving connections root in the same soil, we are wise to tend friendship with uninterrupted devotion. Setting the bar high here keeps it elevated in relationships with family members, with a partner, in the world. Boomerang.

My orientation to the world tips in love's favor. It's the first look I give to the day and, on my best days, love's gaze stays with me. Outgrowing the assumption that negativity is hip, somehow "more real . . . than positive thinking," I "accept and affirm" (*All*

About Love) as my first inclination. Though I career off course, berating myself and lashing out, I return to practice, forever my own housekeeper. Yes, in order "to actualize love it is useful to see it as a practice" (*All About Love*). A tireless laborer for more discussions of love, hooks succeeds in evoking live-wired commentaries everywhere. College students note that she refers to a number of sources in *All About Love*, proving that "love's not set once and for all, and an original thought is unlikely." They marvel at the "weird reluctance" surrounding talk of love, sure that they wouldn't stand for such a haphazard approach to an analysis of education, decision making, or courage. Diners toast yet another confirmation of the limits of language, the inadequacy of "a little definition for a big _____." They appreciate hook's active participation as one who misunderstood love and now models the value of philosophical inquiry, "even, I mean especially about this topic."

Love as action rather than noun—a thing—attracts children for various reasons: "Now I understand what a verb is!" "Being told I'm 'full of myself' turns out to be a compliment. It just depends how full and of what." While adults may debate what hooks means by "spiritual growth," child philosophers explain that "it means your innards puff out." To doubters who decry people's general inability to know what's best for them, much less for another, a fifth grader's incredulity hits the mark: "Well, who would pick gloominess, bad health, jail, and always being lonely if they knew they had a choice?"

Diners' handwritten notes passed for all to see testify that love "generates strength," "completes your essence," "confirms belonging," "satisfies innate thirst," "serves as a catalyst for change," "achieves oneness," "assures survival." "When it works, everything works." Who wouldn't want to dance this two-step?

(P.S. Dratted hard chapter to write, but got some good housecleaning done.)

AND YOUR TOPIC FOR DINNER CONVERSATION IS

"Most folks were just frightened of what might be revealed in any exploration of what love might mean in their lives" (*All About Love*). But not you—not now. Have at it!

THE DOORBELL RINGS

Guests spread the love by bringing something from their own kitchens to the picnic—a family favorite, Grandmother's famous pound cake, or a trusty standby. Diners can provide sweetened and unsweetened iced tea. Tea, a staple element in all sorts of southern cocktails, easily transforms into aptly named "tea punch" with the addition of Kentucky bourbon and a few splashes of bitters.

"Come On-A My House," Rosemary Clooney invites the gang, enjoy some "Mangos" and "eat up and drink up," one and all, "In the Cool, Cool, Cool of the Evening." The Reel World String Band blows in on an *Appalachian Wind*, issuing a raucous "Henhouse Lament" complemented by "Peace and Harmony." This group knows "Where, Kentucky's Blue Moon Rose," tastes "Kentucky Blackberry Blossom," and implores, "Bury Me in Bluegrass." Cellist Ben Sollee flips the kickstand on his bicycle, leaving behind a "Cluttered Mind" and looking for "A Few Honest Words." He sings and strums about the "Prettiest Tree on the Mountain" and "How to See the Sun Rise." Who better than the "Coal Miner's Daughter," Loretta Lynn, to escort you into your discussion? As you assemble, listen to the "Blue Kentucky Girl" from Butcher Hollow tell you the "Story of My Life." Relax "High on a Mountain Top" where "we're high on life and rich in love." Meet Loretta's mama, the "Van Lear Rose," the "belle of Johnson County" who picked Loretta's daddy out of a crowd of adoring miners.

Two musicians softly accompany your conversation. When you hear Helen Humes perform *Songs I Like to Sing*, you'll understand why she was given the key to Louisville. Longtime vocalist with the Count Basie Orchestra, she asks "If I Could Be with You (One Hour Tonight)." Pianist Les McCann introduces you to "Benjamin" and "Roberta" while putting up "Love for Sale." He suggests "Frankly Speaking" as you look for "The Truth." McCann's introspective, hypnotic confession that he "Loved You Full in Every Way" brings your talk home. Wind down with McCann and Eddie Harris on sax in their incomparable "Compared to What."

Loretta Lynn's younger sister wants to party, too. Crystal Gayle switches moods from "Don't It Make My Brown Eyes Blue" to "You Never Gave Up on Me." Off the blanket and on your feet! Sam Bush switches his trademark mandolin for a fiddling salute to "Big Mon," Bill Monroe, the Father of Bluegrass. Trade tunes between generations, alternating takes of Bush's "newgrass" and Monroe's pioneering compositions. Go, Bill!: "Honky Tonk Swing," "Orange Blossom Special," "Kentucky Waltz," "Blue Grass Stomp." Sam admits that Monroe runs *Circles Around Me* but keeps up with "Apple Blossom," "Blue Mountain," "Spooky Lane," "Hungry For Your Love." Big Mon departs, looking up at a "Blue Moon of Kentucky" and his admirer cheers "Roll On Buddy, Roll On."

In the Kitchen

HAM BISCUITS

"Good food is always a trouble and its pre-paration should be regarded as a labor of love . . ." (*French Country Cooking*). Tempted by the treat-filled apron pockets of her "Big Mama," hooks enjoyed busy kitchens crowded with talented cooks working their magic with "a pinch of this and a pinch of that" (*Bone Black: Memories of Girlhood*), soon delivering platters of loving "trouble" to the table. Individually shaped ham biscuits prove just the right picnic provisions for an outing with hooks and friends.

PREPARATION: 45 minutes (35 minutes active)

Butter for greasing the baking sheets

2 cups all-purpose flour

2 teaspoons baking powder

¼ teaspoon baking soda

1 teaspoon salt

6 tablespoons cold, unsalted butter, cut into pea-sized cubes

2 tablespoons solid vegetable shortening

⅓ cup buttermilk

¾ pound thinly sliced cooked country ham

1. Preheat the oven to 450 degrees. Grease two baking sheets with butter and set aside.

2. In a large bowl, sift together the flour, baking powder, baking soda, and salt.

Toss the cubes of butter into the flour to separate and coat. Add the shortening. Using your fingers, work the butter and shortening into the flour mixture by squeezing them between your thumb and fingers until well distributed throughout the flour. The flour should have the texture of cornmeal.

3. Pour in the buttermilk and stir with a fork to incorporate.

4. On a lightly floured surface, pat the dough into a 1-inch-thick rectangle. Knead the dough until lightly mixed; do not overwork.

5. Using a rolling pin, roll out the dough to ½ inch thickness. Use a 2-inch diameter cookie cutter or drinking glass to cut out biscuits. Gather the scraps, reroll the dough, and repeat. Transfer the biscuits to the prepared baking sheets. Expect to have about 20 biscuits.

6. Bake for 8 to 10 minutes, until just beginning to brown. Cool, and then fill with the desired quantity of ham.

CORN SALAD

From the neat rows of her grandmother Baba's backyard plot to mismatched pots perched on urban windowsills, hooks's encounters with gardening reveal "what earth will give when tended lovingly" (*Belonging: A Culture of Place*). Summer corn! Group corn shucking made time for chatter as family lore passed around back porches, with hands small and large at work, husks and silks softly falling away. Use the freshest corn available in making this sturdy picnic salad.

PREPARATION: 1 hour

6 bacon slices

3 plum tomatoes, halved, seeded, and diced

2 tablespoons white balsamic vinegar

1 teaspoon kosher salt

2 tablespoons extra virgin olive oil

4 cups of fresh corn kernels, scraped from 8-10 ears (or 4 cups frozen corn kernels, thawed according to package directions, and drained)

1 large clove garlic, peeled and minced

½ cup chopped fresh basil

1. Cook the bacon in a skillet over low to medium heat until crisp. Drain on paper towels, chop, and set aside.

2. In a medium serving bowl, combine the tomatoes, vinegar, and salt and let sit for 5 to 10 minutes.

3. Heat the oil over medium-high heat in a medium skillet and add the corn and garlic. Cook, stirring, for 2 to 3 minutes. Cool slightly.

4. Add the corn mixture to the tomatoes and stir to combine. Add the bacon and the basil. Serve.

PEACH HAND PIES

Ah, the smell of a freshly baked pie. Wafting aromas of sugary fruit and buttery crust serve as invitations. Imagine generations of quick, confident cooks patting mounds of dough into plentiful small pouches containing luscious fruit. These peach pies take shape into individual hand-sized envelopes just right for the caramelized fruit filling tucked within. Although they travel well, these treats may not make it to the picnic blanket!

PREPARATION: 2 hours, 30 minutes (1 hour active)

CRUST

2½ cups all-purpose flour

2 tablespoons sugar

½ teaspoon salt

1 cup (2 sticks) cold unsalted butter, cut into small cubes

½ cup sour cream

½ cup ice water

FILLING

4–5 peaches, peeled, pitted, and cut into small cubes (substitute jarred or canned peaches if necessary)

2 tablespoons all-purpose flour

1¼ cups sugar, plus extra for dusting finished pies

½ cup heavy cream

3 tablespoons unsalted butter

2 tablespoons light corn syrup

2 teaspoons bourbon

2 large egg yolks mixed with 2 tablespoons cold water

1. In a food processor, combine the flour, sugar, and salt. Add the butter and pulse until just combined. Whisk together the sour cream and ice water. Add to the food processor and pulse briefly. Form the dough into 2 balls, cover with plastic wrap, and refrigerate for 1 hour.

2. Line baking sheets with parchment paper.

3. With a rolling pin, roll each dough half to ⅛ inch thick. Using a 4-inch-diameter round cookie cutter, cut circles out of the dough, rerolling the scraps, and repeating as necessary. Expect around 16–20 circles. Place the circles on the prepared baking sheets and refrigerate for 30 minutes.

4. Meanwhile, make the filling. Toss the peaches with the flour and ½ cup of the sugar and set aside.

5. In a small saucepan over medium heat, bring the cream and butter to a boil and set aside.

6. In a medium saucepan, combine the remaining ¾ cup sugar, the corn syrup, and 2 tablespoons of water, and bring to a boil over medium heat, stirring, until the sugar dissolves. Continue to boil over medium heat, without stirring, until the mixture is a light caramel color. Carefully (it will splatter) pour in the cream mixture and add the bourbon, and continue to cook, stirring, until the mixture begins to thicken, approximately 5 minutes. Transfer the caramel sauce to a heatproof container.

7. Preheat the oven to 375 degrees.

8. Assemble the hand pies. Drain any excess liquid from the peach mixture. Place a generous tablespoon of the mixture in the center of each dough circle, followed by a dollop of caramel. If the caramel has become too stiff to work with, rewarm until softened. Brush the edges of the circles with water and fold over to make half-moon shapes. Use a fork to crimp the edges and seal. Brush the pies with the egg yolk and water mixture and sprinkle generously with sugar. Bake for 20 to 25 minutes, until nicely browned. Cool on wire rack.

KENTUCKY TO GO

Hear powerful black voices in Frank X Walker's poems of *Affrilachia*, and "black country girl" Crystal Wilkinson's *Water Street* and *Blackberries, Blackberries*. . . . Jam with fiddlers at J. P. Fraley's Mountain Music Gathering, wear the colors of college basketball's Hilltoppers, Wildcats, or Cardinals, and clap for Ashland's baseball all-star Brandon Webb and hometown girls Naomi and Wynonna Judd's "Girls Night Out." . . . Wind along the Lincoln Heritage Scenic Highway, stopping in Hodgenville and Abraham Lincoln's Knob Creek boyhood home. . . . Plan a sleepover in Maysville for its Music Festival, founded by Rosemary Clooney, and linger the next day for a detailed tour of the Bierbower House with its compelling National Underground Railroad Museum. . . . Experience the Bluegrass State through early, raw *Mountain Music of Ken-*

tucky, as the Old Regular Baptist Church chants "Amazing Grace" and, years later, ask with Joan Osborne if God is "One of Us." . . .

RESOURCES

PHILOSOPHY

All About Love by bell hooks.

MUSIC

Essential Rosemary Clooney by Rosemary Clooney: "Come On-A My House," "Mangos," "In the Cool, Cool, Cool of the Evening."

Appalachian Wind by Reel World String Band: "Appalachian Wind," "Henhouse Lament," "Peace and Harmony."

Live Music by Reel World String Band: "Where Kentucky's Blue Moon Rose," "Kentucky Blackberry Blossom," "Bury Me in Bluegrass."

Inclusions by Ben Sollee: "Cluttered Mind."

Learning to Bend by Ben Sollee: "A Few Honest Words," "Prettiest Tree on the Mountain," "How to See the Sun Rise."

Definitive Collection by Loretta Lynn: "Blue Kentucky Girl."

Van Lear Rose by Loretta Lynn: "Story of My Life," "High on a Mountain Top," "Van Lear Rose."

Songs I Like to Sing! by Helen Humes: "If I Could Be with You (One Hour Tonight)."

Much Les by Les McCann: "Benjamin," "Roberta," "Love for Sale."

The Truth (The Whole Truth & Nothing But the Truth) by Les McCann: "Frankly Speaking," "The Truth."

Talk to the People / River High River Low by Les McCann: "Loved You Full in Every Way."

Swiss Movement by Les McCann and Eddie Harris: "Compared to What."

Crystal Gayle: The Hits by Crystal Gayle: "Don't It Make My Brown Eyes Blue," "You Never Gave Up on Me."

All the Classic Releases 1937–1949 by Bill Monroe: "Honky Tonk Swing," "Orange Blossom Special," "Kentucky Waltz," "Blue Grass Stomp," "Blue Moon of Kentucky."

Ice Caps: Peaks of Telluride by Sam Bush: "Big Mon," "Spooky Lane," "Hungry for Your Love."

Circles Around Me by Sam Bush: "Apple Blossom," "Blue Mountain," "Roll On Buddy, Roll On."

FOOD

French Country Cooking by Elizabeth David.

Bone Black: Memories of Girlhood by bell hooks.

Belonging: A Culture of Place by bell hooks.

A Fruitful Ecological Solution

SEPTEMBER IN KENYA

The photograph's caption would read "The Bagel Dance." As I set out toward the classroom from my office, my student bore down upon me at a fast clip from the opposite direction. He trapped his ethics text under an elbow, and his other arm waved an oddly menacing bagel my way. We collided at the bustling intersection of two hallways, and while students and faculty swept past, time stopped for us. No uniformed athlete could surpass his blocking ability. An earnest student who was growing more disconsolate with each class

discussion of environmental issues, he demanded: "What right do I have to be eating this breakfast when others go hungry? How can *you* justify *that*?" He foiled my every maneuver aimed at herding us both to class. First, I asked who would be helped if he chose not to eat his still-hot bagel. What would he do with it? He parried my shoulder shake left and stood his ground. Next, I told him about my neighbor's organic bagel business. Interest flickered but he wasn't fooled by my head shake right. Then, I suggested that he come to class, learn more about the issues, and talk with classmates about practical ways to address the ecological damage that causes hunger. His slight defensive crouch straightened at last. "Walk with me—if you want, feel free to leave after fifteen minutes," I invited him. We walked. He stayed.

No topic overwhelms quite like this one. Knowing the magnitude of ecological destruction can freeze anyone in their tracks. What do we do when we're made aware of problems such as mountaintop coal removal, its endless downstream and airborne pollution further complicated by the greenhouse gas emissions released from the burning coal . . . "fracking," the process of hydraulic underground drilling for shale gas with its promise of cheaper energy won at the expense of water contamination . . . where to store radioactive waste and the overarching question of nuclear facilities themselves . . . the damage inflicted upon indigenous peoples, from Ecuador to India, by industrial development . . . the dangers of genetically modified food? Worried faces around dinner tables talk through local issues, such as runoff contaminants from a pulp mill that are killing the water-filtering mussel. A debate among electric company officials, environmentalists, and legislators over the use of wind turbines, which will spell certain doom for many bird species, ends in the go-ahead for a New Hampshire project but the rejection of a similar one in southwest Washington. Wherever I go I can expect talk about the Keystone XL oil pipeline project, which (if approved) extracts crude oil from Canada's tar sands and pipes it across the United States for refinery, fuel, and job creation at the expense of incalculable energy and an unthinkable victory of carbon over oxygen. But: A mass of approximately twelve thousand people surrounded the White House on November 6, 2011, to protest the pipeline, thrusting the pros and cons into widespread and ongoing public discussion. That protest was the culmination of much smaller, local efforts. Indeed each of the above issues encounters stiff opposition. Diners realize what my stuck student learned with time—ecological awareness and progress is well under way. Knowledge is essential and serves as incentive. What we don't know *will* hurt us.

No topic motivates quite like this one. As Sean insisted at semester's beginning and end, "If we don't address ecological issues, we won't have any others." Many individual and group initiatives undertaken by his classmates, and with his energetic participation, restored my bagel-dance partner's hope. One Saturday was spent working at a wildlife sanctuary, another creating an outdoor classroom at an elementary school. Animal rescue, river cleanup, restoring homes, free bicycle repair—and the list goes on. Amber presented each classmate with a native dogwood seedling, giving many their first experience with planting and tending. Dan assumed the role of a very public investigator of the college's recycling protocol, from computing lab to cafe-

teria, and questioned the rationale for every felled tree. Neal joined a group in fashioning raised beds on campus, transforming an unused, mowed area into a biodiverse garden of vegetables, herbs, and flowers fed by an organic compost pile. "I would consider it theft if anyone took away ingredients that contribute to composting. Look at these lush plants!" Imagine reporting robbery of leaves, grass clippings, sticks, apple cores, wilted lettuce, and banana peels! Much of this produce was given away while the rest was savored by the campus growers. We work within the circumstances of our lives.

No topic generates more abiding commitment than this one. Elementary and college students, along with diners, discover that involvement with the natural world, once begun, is irresistible. When we lack this vital reconnection (or first connection), the planet's woes remain abstract. Contact with the earth brings the problems, and us, home. If I had to name the most significant event in my years as a college professor, it would be the planting of a campus garden in my grandmother's memory. As a dirty-kneed, wheelbarrow-crashing child at work with my grandfather in his backyard plot, I picked from rows (eternal) of string and butter beans, tasted homegrown tomatoes, spinach, onions, kale, cucumbers, potatoes, and surprise treats cooked inside sugar pumpkins. That gut-level relationship to dirt and its rewards flooded my heart again as my students and I spread organic matter at the base of two established trees, which struggled for water in poor soil, and we buried the first bulbs. Families, friends, colleagues, and passersby joined us as the garden shaped itself over the years: Free-standing soapstone benches and rock stools, beech and redbud trees, rosemary and mint, a picnic table made from recycled plastic, birds perched at feeders, mountain views and inner satisfaction. Here the college community gathers, students return to celebrate their ensuing graduations, visitors spread a picnic, and potential hires answer interview questions.

Diners respond to this garden with similarly joyful tales. Like me, their barefoot-childhood connection had diminished over time, but oh, the addictive pleasure when restored: Employees start a community vegetable garden at the workplace, also planting shade trees on an open hillside; residents of a big-city apartment complex add clusters of natural grasses and shrubs to an existing stand of trees, crafting park benches for their evening roosting; volunteers at botanical gardens can't get enough, inviting school groups and senior centers for tours; staff members rave about their restaurant rooftop herb and vegetable gardens, giving takeout samples for guests to root in sunny windowsills; dinner hosts buy a small share in the farmers' co-op, reaping weekly produce pickups.

Kenya's Wangari Maathai (wan-GAH-ree ma-THIGH) stands tall among the fifty-some million trees thriving under the thumb of her Green Belt Movement. In my experience, no philosopher is more cherished by those who read her work, hear her speak, and mark her life. Gently, fiercely, physically, spiritually, she educates and inspires. Trees are us. You'll see.

PREPPING FOR KENYA

Read culinary guru Binyavanga Wainaina's promise that *One Day I Will Write About This Place*, listen to the plucking of the Luo tribe's *nyatiti* (eight-stringed lyre), trace track star Kip Keino's athletic and philanthropic legacy, and stop for "Lunch Time" serenaded by Gabriel Omolo. . . . Visit the Maasai Mara National Reserve to witness the Great Wildebeest Migration and to admire hippo, crocodile, gazelle, and zebra. . . . After strolling through historic Lamu Old Town, near Mombasa, stretch out on the white beaches of the Indian Ocean, and soon set a date with the blue monkeys to climb Buyango Hill in tropical Kakamega Forest. . . . Look into the women's eyes staring from the walls of the Kibera slums in the provocative photographic/graffiti installation by French artist JR. . . . Join more than 25,000 participants in the Mathare Youth Sports Association, cleaning fields for soccer games, paying team dues with community service, scoring big goals by earning scholarships. . . . Learn to read with Kimani N'gan'ga Maruge in Justin Chadwick's rousing film *The First Grader*. . . .

INDEED, IN MY MORE FANCIFUL MOMENTS I CONCEIVE OF THE TREE AS AN UPSIDE-DOWN PERSON, WITH HER HEAD IN THE SOIL AND FEET AND LEGS IN THE AIR. THE TREE USES ITS ROOTS TO EAT AND ITS LEAVES TO BREATHE. . . .

WANGARI MAATHAI,
Replenishing the Earth

A little girl farming in the small village of Ithithe with her Kikuyu tribe family became the first woman to earn a doctorate in all of central and eastern Africa. But hardships suffered by rural Kenyan women called Dr. Maathai away from her University of Nairobi professorship in Anatomy and Animal Science. Malnutrition, poverty, and tribal fighting over scant resources motivated her to find a solution. "Why not plant trees?" which would secure firewood, fencing, "shade for humans and animals, protect watersheds and bind the soil, and if they were fruit trees, provide food. They would also heal the land . . . and regenerate the vitality of the earth" (*Unbowed*). Aware and uncaring that many would find her reverence for trees foolish and backward, she endured police beatings and imprisonments in successful protests against high-rise construction in Uhuru Park and sale of parcels of Karura Forest. Her husband divorced her, correct in his assessment that she was smart, uncontrollable, and powerful. Among the founders of the Forum for the Restoration of Democracy, she was awarded the Jane Addams Leadership Award in 1993, and in 2004, the Nobel Peace Prize. We dig.

TAKING

In the shadow of her beloved Mount Kenya, Maathai watched the richness of communal life, lived from and on the land, disappear. Soil lost its nutrients and water its purity because of massive deforestation, and without firewood even the simplest food could not be prepared. She understood that no one set out deliberately to cause either the Kenyan or planetary ecological scourge. Nearsightedness induced climate change and species' extinctions. She invites us to "address the attitudes that lead us to such self-destruction" (*Replenishing the Earth*). While we react to crises, their causes lie tucked inside our worldviews. A sampling of traditional Kikuyu values proves a smart place to begin our attitude assessment—and hopefully to return.

Consider: Intimately entwined within the natural world, community members extol and instill the virtues of gratitude, generosity, hard work, and thrift. Gratitude for the earth's bounty forges Kikuyu relationships—with deep appreciation for nature's provisions, the heart opens in thanksgiving to the earth and its inhabitants. Amidst harvests of fruits and vegetables supplemented by neighborly generosity, hospitality develops automatically. Opportunities for sharing food and shelter are welcomed. Everyone antes up, paying respect to the land with hard work and discipline. Positive attributes such as thrift, far from implying want, assure "wise, thoughtful accumulation" (*Replenishing*). Enough is enough. Restraint serves as faithful guide Waste insults.

Contrast: Astronauts write emotionally about their life-altering experiences witnessing the earth from space. One planet enfolds everything within its intricate maze. Nothing *can* be set apart from or unaffected by *anything* else. Up close, however, we wear blindfolds. Wrought by industrialization, urban living, and habitat loss, exploitation wins when the split between humans and nature occurs. A student drives a truck averaging seven miles to the gallon: "I can afford it." A state official dispatches chainsaws after a swath of old trees so the new addition to campus will be visible from the interstate: "I got it built." Oversized vehicles line up, engines running, parents chatting: "I don't want my child to wait." A contractor digs a trench ten feet from a nearby tree that twenty-five feet would have spared: "I saved money on pipe." Diners mull bedeviling tradeoffs: benefits of a fish diet coupled with ruinous oceanic conditions due to overfishing; the impeccable conservation of Costa Rica's Monteverde cloud forest no match for mist evaporation caused by deforestation below, though the cutting provides desperately needed jobs; wood-burning stoves save fossil fuels but emit gaseous carbon; disposal of electric car batteries poses huge toxic risks. Yes! Scrap together with uncomfortable topics, Maathai encourages, because awareness changes mindsets and lifestyles. Yes, we'll always take from the world, and to some extent tradeoffs are inevitable. But we can trade up because "we can love ourselves by loving the earth . . ." (*Replenishing*). Children embrace her: "We're all up the river from somebody." "She's the only philosopher who knows the world is a tree house."

The shift begins as we relearn ways of assigning value other than monetary. "Can we really put a price tag on the carbon dioxide trees capture" (*Replenishing*), the oxygen and water provided? Imagine a way of life suggested by the Kikuyu gourd tradition. After accepting the gift of a gourd brimming with porridge or beer, the recipient carefully oils the gourd before returning it. Over time and travel, the gourd's rich, dark sheen and velvety feel, varnished by repeated acts of generosity, swell the giver's heart. Passing from Maathai's hands to ours, "we could benefit from spending more time polishing our gourds for one another . . ." (*Replenishing*). Neither new-age nor old-fashioned, Maathai boldly challenges us to ask: "Is our time spent fruitfully? Are we living a life that . . . is all we had hoped it would be" (*Replenishing*)? Wealth belongs to givers.

GIVING

Once philosophers' investigations reveal the "what" of ecological damage, this knowledge pops the bubble of passivity and piques resolve to figure out the "how" of solutions. The paralyzing sense of "too little, too late" (*Replenishing*) gives way to action. We may not have known, but now we do. "In the end, all we are called to do is the best we can" (*Replenishing*).

Maathai prompts diners with her tips: Use public, foot, and leg transportation; energy-efficient lightbulbs and appliances;

harvested rainwater and both sides of re-cycled paper; quality insulation and caulk, white paint for rooftops and reusable chop-sticks; ever-lessening amounts of water and electricity; and no plastic bags.

Okay!

Philosophy circles testify to thermostats turned lower in winter and higher in sum-mer, billowing warm weather clotheslines, sun-brewed tea, natural grasses and wild-flowers replacing mown grass. A carpenter passes along his discovery of nonhazardous glues and finishes. Philosophers wow one another at a retirement center where enthu-siasts grow and tend rare species of differ-ing flowers, their show-and-tell sessions providing group pleasure and education. Maturing butterfly gardens and bird sanctu-aries accommodate winged residents and tiptoeing children. Advocacy and collabora-tion succeed. Landowners take advice from foresters; petitions for safe bike lanes and sidewalks mapped out by college engineer-ing students sail through local govern-ments; demands for public transportation strengthen in numbers and efficacy; com-munities sign up for single-stream sorting for recycling, making this service cheaper, and eco-unfriendly garbage collection in-creasingly expensive; organizations scour high school and college concerts and games, passing out recycling bags and information; store owners stock and promote local foods.

Look at diners happily competing to "look at the problem in front of you and try to solve it" (*Replenishing*). If public transpor-tation isn't feasible, carpools rule. They dress for the weather, muting heat pumps and furnaces. Glass jugs, "growlers," trans-port beer, "better brew, better price, one container." Worn bags (perhaps one day we can all use traditional Kenyan baskets woven from the sustainable sisal plant, ex-ported by the millions via fair trade) carry groceries for diners fast becoming more dis-cerning shoppers. This pineapple traveled to Vermont in January? Why three separate plastic wrappings? Processed food labels receive small print scrutiny. Pricey items inspire homegrown efforts: winter window boxes and summer gardens reap basil and flowers, figs and elderberries, asparagus and melons, spicy and bell peppers, heirloom tomatoes grown from seeds purchased at the hardware store. Fabric napkins mop chins—guests stash leftovers in glass storage containers with air-locking lids.

"It's a sobering thought that if the human species were to become extinct, no species that I know of would die out because we were not there to sustain them. Yet if some of them became extinct human beings would also die out" (*Replenishing*). Trees give us breath. We suffocate without them. At Maathai's insistence, we beam our attention on the single entity best able to turn the environmental tide. We rely on "the power of the tree" (*Replenishing*). So, we plant.

Invite a tree expert to dinner. Lack of knowledge often stymies would-be planters, while good information pushes hesitators outdoors. Jacob galvanized one dinner group, and even veteran arborists took away new ideas that they scribbled on scrap paper. Start with questions. Is the tree suitable for your climate and a particular space? Will this or will that spot return the most benefit, mindful that shade trees should be planted on the west side of the house to block summer's intense afternoon sun, and an evergreen windscreen protects from wintry blasts. Think about privacy versus blocking a view. How about a fruit-bearing tree, doubling the pleasure? Jacob's love for trees diffused any intimidation. No matter the tree(s) selected, a few universal hints apply: At the nursery, choose trees with the best branch structures, smallest wounds, and healthy root flares. Detangle bound up root balls. Dig the "perfect hole," sufficiently wide and deep for the tree you're planting, and mix in plenty of decomposed organic matter. Water frequently—initial care is crucial. Prune early for structure and shape to avoid eventual expensive and perhaps futile bracing and cabling. Clip off any potentially problematic branches, literally "nipping them in the bud," so that the bud never sprouts. Resources abound. For example, the Arbor Day Foundation offers new members ten (free) tree seedlings appropriate for their areas. Tree planting replenishes human spirit as it restores the earth's "cloth of green" (*Unbowed*). Shovels, pickaxes, coworkers, and neighbors at the ready, diners set out. We breathe more easily as we dig.

Hers was not a look back to a glorious, illusive past. Maathai benefitted from electricity and education, and her Nobel Prize (celebrated by her planting a Nandi flame tree) set her on a globe-spinning schedule. Driven by compassion and justice and grounded firmly in hard science, she spread local and global blankets of action-inducing knowledge, seeking to unite people everywhere in changing course and heading in a wise, for All, direction. How she gladdened whenever she saw the fulfillment of a project, brown and despoiled soil turned green

and fertile. Such progress as she watched the thick, expanding waistline of her now-international Green Belt Movement reflected in the regreening of Israel's Negev and China's Gobi Deserts, and African nations connecting in the Great Green Wall project, an extra-large belt of trees planned for a five-thousand mile long, nine-mile-wide stretch in the Sahara Desert. When the Kenyan army joins forces with Green Belters, keeping peace among ethnic groups by waging war against desertification, the sky no longer seems the limit. How could the laughing woman, comparing herself to the hummingbird trying its best to put out a forest fire one tiny droplet at a time, foresee likeminded Russian protesters of tree removal camping in the Khimki Forest?

When thinking about writing this book, exploring and sharing Dr. Maathai's life's work excited me most. She gives us new ears for listening, reassurance that "we are in the company of many others throughout the world who care deeply about this blue planet" (*Unbowed*), and the heart to try. She teaches us all to say that "after all I was a child of the same soil" (*Unbowed*). Wangari Maathai died in late September 2011, an ideal time for tree planting.

The Kikuyu have a saying to express gratitude at the exchange of gifts: "*Kanya gatune nī mwamūkanīro*" (*Replenishing*). Thank you, generous recycler of wisdom and good works.

~~~~~~~~~~

AND YOUR TOPIC FOR DINNER CONVERSATION IS

"When I raise the issue of the loss of the natural world in the Green Belt Movement's civic and environmental seminars, many participants tell me that it's as if they had looked at the world around them for the first time" (*Replenishing*). Look at the world. What do you see, locally and globally? What ecological issue calls your name? What's your response? One by one, go round the table.

~~~~~~~~~~

THE DOORBELL RINGS

Although typical African dinners do not include an appetizer course, boiled peanuts and grilled plantains are popular street foods, and guests can purchase roasted peanuts and dried plantain (or banana) chips for tasty substitutes. Fresh or dried figs honor Maathai's beloved tree. Diners can bring bottled teas or beer (in Africa, beer bottles are cleaned and refilled after each use). If you feel adventurous, try your hand at making a homemade, African-style beer using millet, ginger, or bananas. Native to southern Africa and one of the continent's best-loved gourds, watermelon provides a refreshing dessert pickup, and be sure to bake or buy a seasonal fruit pie.

Shake to the beat of African rumba in Orchestra Super Mazembe's "Shauri Yako." Carry on to their "Samba" and "Kassongo." Next up, Machito honors *Kenya* with some Afro-Cuban jazz. Bounce along on your visit to "Kenya" and romp through the "Wild Jungle," twitch shoulders to "Oyeme" and "Blues A La Machito," and listen to his "Conversation" while readying for yours. But not before activist Suzzana Owiyo invites you to the centennial party in her rousing "Kisumu 100." Imagine being part of the clapping crowd of some sixty thousand along the shores of Lake Victoria in the port city of Kisumu. Owiyo's "Mama Africa" sweetly turns your attention to your night with Maathai.

Ease into your conversation with pioneering electric guitarist and vocalist Fundi Konde. Meet "Mama Sowera" and "Olivia Leo," sit back with "Elina Ni Wako" and "Fundi Ni Yatima." Welcome your musical introduction to "African Child" by philosopher/environmentalist Lydia Achieng Abura, relaxing with her "Flying High" and "Nifanye Nini." Joseph Muyale conducts The Kenyan Boys Choir to international acclaim following their performance at the festivities surrounding the inauguration of President Obama, in 2009. What an appropriate and lovely backdrop their songs provide for your gathering: "Homeless," "Tuli Tuli," "Kikererani Lelo" ("Kapchesan"), "Jambo Bwana," and "Nkosi Sikelel'i Afrika." An acappella group's self-titled album *Kayamba Africa* rounds out your discussion with their rendition of a traditional song much loved by Maathai's Kikuyu tribe. Welcome the coming rain in "Wakariru."

Chai tea, a delicious boiled blend of milk, sugar, and spices served throughout the day in Africa, lends a soothing touch as the evening's philosophizing lightens up. Kick your shoes off as The Victoria Kings bring the rhythms of *benga*, Kenyan dance music, to the party. Swing to the guitar riffs and cheery vocals of "Eddo! Eddo! #1" and don't stop with "Eddo! Eddo! #2." Bandleader of Orchestra Limpopo International, guitarist, composer, and rumba aficionado Musa Juma sways into the room with "Christina" and "Betty." Juma instigates a bit more fun with "Hera Mudho" and "Aggrey," sending you into a Kenyan night to the tune of "O'yoo Daktari" and with thoughts of a "Safari."

SQUASH AND APPLE SOUP

What's for dinner? From heirloom-seed enthusiasts to farm share members to urban food foragers, diners (finally) know *what* is for dinner. Gathering, cooking, and sharing food has become a powerful setting for fomenting social change. Bicycling activists barter persimmons for plums from backyard fruit trees—in pie "labs," pie makers bring locals together in grassroots initiatives for sustainable living ("Pie + Design = Change," *The New York Times*). Appreciated throughout Africa, winter squash is the most versatile member of the gourd family. Make this smooth soup with local winter squash that has been cultivated for maximum taste rather than for consistent size and shape. If possible visit a nearby pick-your-own apple orchard to discover interesting varieties of pesticide-free apples not available in the grocery, and pluck a few tangy counterpoints to the sweet squash.

PREPARATION: 2 hours, 30 minutes (1 hour active)

3 winter squash (butternut, acorn, kabocha, or similar variety), about 2 pounds each

2 tablespoons canola oil

4 tablespoons (½ stick) unsalted butter

2 Granny Smith, Stayman, Winesap, or other tart apples, peeled, cored, and diced

2 leeks, white parts only, halved, thoroughly rinsed, and coarsely chopped

½ teaspoon ground ginger

½ teaspoon red curry paste

1½ teaspoons salt

1 teaspoon white pepper

2 tablespoons honey

2 quarts chicken or vegetable stock

½ cup crème fraîche, or sour cream

1 bunch of fresh chives, chopped

1. Preheat the oven to 350 degrees. Line two rimmed baking sheets with aluminum foil.

2. Cut the squash in half and scoop out and discard the seeds. If using a variety of squash with a long neck (e.g., butternut), slice the neck off first before halving. Brush the squash halves, including the neck, with the canola oil and place, cut side down, on the baking sheets.

3. Roast for 1 hour, or until completely tender. When cool, scoop out the flesh and set aside.

4. In a large pot over medium heat, melt the butter. Add the apples and leeks and cook, stirring, for 5 minutes. Add the ginger, red curry paste, salt, and pepper, and cook for 3 to 4 minutes. Mix in the honey, then add the stock and bring to a boil.

5. Reduce the heat to a simmer, cover, and cook for 15 minutes. Add the squash and simmer, uncovered, for 10 minutes. Cool.

6. In a blender or a food processor, puree the soup in batches until smooth. Return to the pot and heat over medium-low until just hot. Serve in bowls with a dollop of crème fraîche and sprinkle with the chives.

NO-KNEAD AFRICAN SEED BREAD

The act of bread making takes on new life in the hands of Jim Lahey, the artisanal baker who cultivated his own wild yeast and used it to craft beautiful, rustic rounds of bread that changed the lives of bakers and bread eaters around the world. With a nod to ancient practices, Lahey figured out how he (and you) can create complex loaves of bread by harnessing the power of our most sustainable resource—time. Inspired by South African seed bread, this version is a slow-rise marvel. Before making the bread, try to find time to read Mark Bittman's follow up to his initial publication of Lahey's recipe in *The New York Times*. Bittman's suggested alterations to the original recipe underscore its flexibility—from rise times to pot sizes to flavorings. Begin making the bread the evening before your group's gathering. With 21 hours of total rising time required, this will enable you to bake your bread just before your guests arrive.

PREPARATION: 22 hours (15 minutes active)

3 cups all-purpose flour

¼ teaspoon instant or rapid-rise yeast (regular yeast will not work)

2½ teaspoons salt

1½ cups water

2–3 tablespoons raw sunflower seeds

2–3 tablespoons sesame seeds

1. In a large bowl, combine the flour, yeast, and salt. Add 1½ cups of water and stir with a wooden spoon until combined. Stir in the sunflower and sesame seeds to distribute. Cover the bowl with plastic wrap and allow the dough to rise at room temperature for 18 hours, or until the dough's surface is bubbly.

2. The dough will be sticky, so be sure to coat your hands with flour before han-

dling. Turn the dough out onto a floured surface and fold over once or twice, sprinkling flour on the dough as necessary. Cover with plastic wrap and allow the dough to rest for 15 minutes. Working quickly with floured hands, shape the dough into a ball by rounding the dough in your hands and working the sides of the dough to the bottom. Squeeze and pinch the dough together on the bottom of the ball to form a seam. Place the dough, seam side down, on a lightly floured surface (such as a cutting board) and cover lightly with a cloth napkin or tea towel. Allow the dough to rise (in a warm spot, not cold counter) for 2 to 3 hours, until approximately doubled in bulk.

3. When the dough has risen, place a 3- to 4-quart heavy pot (a larger pot will result in lower cooked loaf height) with a heatproof lid in a cold oven and preheat to 450 degrees. Remove the pot from the oven when hot.

4. Place the dough in the pot, seam side up. Cover the pot with the lid and bake for 30 minutes. Remove the lid after 30 minutes and continue to bake until the loaf is nicely browned, 15 to 30 minutes. Run a knife around the edge of the pot and remove the bread round. Cool on a wire rack.

KENYA TO GO

Watch Maathai identify with the hummingbird in *Dirt! The Movie*, directed by Bill Benenson and Gene Rosow. . . . Tour Nairobi, its University, river banks, National Park, and remember to look up at Mount Kenya. . . . Check out the foundation established in memory of photojournalist Mohamed Amin and run alongside champion marathoner Catherine Ndereba as she passes the baton to Florence Kiplagat and 2012 Gold Medal Olympian David Rudisha. . . . Dine with Owuor, portrayed by Sidede Onyulo, in Caroline Link's *Nowhere in Africa*, study the Mau Mau Rebellion, and read Ngũgĩ wa Thiong'o's *Petals of Blood* and *Wizard of the Crow*. . . . Travel along the Great Rift Valley's Elgeyo Escarpment and walk with paleontologists Kamoya Kimeu and Richard Leakey to the site of their fossil recovery of the 1.6-million-year-old (old!) boy at Lake Turkana. . . . Read *Bill Bryson's African Diary*, his book and trek through Kenya supported by CARE International, and get to know the refugees fleeing to Dadaab. . . .

RESOURCES

PHILOSOPHY

Replenishing the Earth by Wangari Maathai

Unbowed by Wangari Maathai

MUSIC

Giants of East Africa by Orchestra Super Mazembe: "Shauri Yako," "Samba," "Kassongo."

Kenya by Machito: "Kenya," "Wild Jungle," "Oyeme," "Blues A La Machito," "Conversation."

Mama Africa by Suzzana Owiyo: "Kisumu 100," "Mama Africa."

Retrospective Volume One: 1947–1956 by Fundi Konde: "Mama Sowera," "Olivia Leo," "Elina Ni Wako," "Fundi Ni Yatima."

Dhahabu Yangu by Lydia Achieng Abura: "African Child," "Flying High," "Nifanye Nini."

Spirit of Africa by The Kenyan Boys Choir: "Homeless," "Tuli Tuli," "Kikererani Lelo" ("Kapchesan"), "Jambo Bwana," "Nkosi Sikelel'i Afrika."

Kayamba Africa by Kayamba Africa: "Wakariru."

The Mighty Kings of Benga by The Victoria Kings: "Eddo! Eddo! #1," "Eddo! Eddo! #2."

Freddy by Musa Juma & Limpopo International: "Christina."

Maselina by Musa Juma: "Betty," "Hera Mudho," "Safari."

Fiance by Musa Juma: "Aggrey," "O'yoo Daktari."

FOOD

"Pie + Design = Change" by John T. Edge, *The New York Times*, October 8, 2010.

My Bread: The Revolutionary No-Work, No-Knead Method by Jim Lahey, with Rick Flaste.

"No Kneading, but Some Fine-Tuning" by Mark Bittman, *The New York Times*, December 6, 2006.

The Africa Cookbook: Tastes of a Continent by Jessica B. Harris.

Rational Decision Making

OCTOBER IN GERMANY

Question: Is x a negative number? Answer: That depends on what x is. Question: Is $(x + y)^2$ the same as $x^2 + y^2$? Answer: No. $(x + y)^2 = x^2 + 2xy + y^2$.

I grew accustomed to and occasionally envious of such student-teacher exchanges during years of office-sharing with a math professor. How different were those interactions, using calculators and following the "order of operations," from the interactions across the small room between my philosophy students and me. Questions: Should I transfer to a college out of state that offers the degree in kinesiology that matches my career goals, if my grandparents living here

depend on my help? My gay teenager endures taunting threats at school, but he begs me not to talk to the principal. I fear for his safety and must act, yet worry about losing his trust. What would you do? I omitted a minor criminal offence from my job application because I thought it would rule out my chances. Now that I've been hired and things are going well, should I come clean with my boss? Answer to all of the above: I don't know.

As students of philosophy sharpen their powers of observation and analysis, they develop an increasing ability to articulate ethical problems. Pros and cons, pain here versus pleasure there, personal desires weighed against other responsibilities, opposing alternatives freeze the decision-making process. Rather than one correct solution to an issue, contrasting possibilities, all with pluses and minuses, present themselves. Though philosophy books have no answers in the back, I never hear these oft-asked queries posed by math students: "Why do I need this?" "How will I use this knowledge in real life?" Budding philosophers know that they are developing essential skills for good living. Mental clarity is their ally, but at times clear thinking creates tension by revealing previously hidden conflicts and increasing uncertainty amongst mounting possibilities. "What ifs" everywhere.

Who looks forward to decision making? Does anyone find it easy to draw the line, do the deed, and no turning back? Think of our waffling ways over the slightest things. What to pack? Where to park? Which day to do laundry? Walk now or later? Not only choosing a movie, but the time, too? This toothpaste . . . that furniture arrangement . . . your place or mine? Window or aisle—maybe I'll stand. Tell the waiter he erred in your favor (only a buck) if the service was poor? Commitment proves elusive. Why? What if you pack for the wrong weather conditions, dislike the movie, and the suddenly attentive waiter follows you to the car? So what? Even in these tiny matters, responsibility sticks, like glue, to every choice. Be gone, persistent burden of ownership. Why carry it?

Yes, it's the awareness of responsibility that forms lines outside my college office and causes diners to linger long after dessert. Heavy complications abound as a dilemma's deadline looms, someone loses no matter what, and failure to choose nevertheless constitutes a choice. Predicaments demand action, though. Should I disclose to the judge a missing piece of information if it might free the accused I believe to be guilty? Dare I talk to the physician about my father's health without my dad's consent?

What happens to the employee who fights against workplace harassment or brings pay inequity to light? Given the company's public record of environmental abuses, am I implicated as a shareholder? Though I promised to attend my child's recital, the overtime cash I can earn that evening will pay for many more piano lessons, so . . . ? Is it my place to ask my partner to seek, or to discontinue, medical treatment? Will I regret intervening? Too much, my cohorts in indecision agree. How to proceed and become a master decision maker? Step by step.

Accepting the inevitability of a lifetime of choices marks a good first step. No matter how fast our feet pedal, forks in the road appear, disappear, and reappear. Thinkers of all ages take comfort in the basic truth that questions—either/or, right/wrong, stay/go, yes/no—will holler at us all our lives. Making decisions is something humans do, like growing up and older, like changing shoe sizes and tastes. The question remains how to pick wisely among competing op-

tions, tugging and pushing, without leaving a trail of "but, but, but."

The next, very long stride forward consists of choosing to view responsibility as an opportunity. Philosophers of all ages like this positive twist. Child philosophers gain self-respect as they consistently hold themselves accountable for behavior on the school bus and at recess, for completing an assignment over the weekend, for seeking help when needed, for saying no when the crowd says yes. More seasoned philosophers speak to this burgeoning sense of self, as well. "I'm maturing by making choices." "I got credit for a hole in one at the charity golf tournament. No one saw my whiff on the first crack at the ball (that barely grazed it), but I told the tournament organizers anyway." "The 'secret' had festered long enough, and now my family can put away the past. Glad I made the move." "I barely recognized my voice as the one challenging the corporation's shoddy practices. I liked the sound of it."

Does $-4^2 = 16$? No. We square and then multiply by negative one, and the answer is -16. Ah, for the assurance provided by this question and answer sequence. Nonetheless I take the last step forward and admit that closure will never wrap itself around hard decisions. Other alternatives did indeed exist—but now I wonder if I really need or even want absolute certainty. How would *that* feel, the world settled once and for all, life a math problem? Does anyone know the answers with complete confidence? Who and where are the authorities? Maybe the triumph for each of us lies in our handling this very uncertainty—here we find our chance to stand firm, choose, and live with it. I can't decide!

Fortunately, most of our decisions are small ones that do not affect other lives. Flip-flops or sneakers, eggs or cereal, stay in or night out, fiction or nonfiction? When faced with impossible situations, however, a strong voice from eighteenth-century Germany reaches our ears. Though he never traveled far from home, Immanuel Kant's (canht) approach to hard choices still exerts worldwide influence. If we use pure reason to think through a problem, intent *only* on doing the right thing for the right reason, the correct solution to the dilemma rises, like cream, to the top. He's hosting us for dinner. Let's see just how sure he is—and how reasonable we are.

PREPPING FOR GERMANY

Listen as *Marlene Dietrich Sings Berlin*, enjoy her starring role in Josef von Sternberg's 1932 classic *Shanghai Express*, and solve the mystery of *M* directed by Fritz Lang. . . . Celebrate the Bavarian tradition of Munich's Oktoberfest, sauntering around the Marienplatz and watching the show at the Glockenspiel. . . . Climb aboard a steamboat for the Rhine in Flames Festival, stopping along the river for the Beethovenfest in Bonn and the illuminated Cathedral of Cologne, where Gerhard Richter's stained glass window dazzles, making note to investigate Richter's Grey Paintings. . . . Catch the familiar rhythm of Kurt Weill's "Mack the Knife" from *The Threepenny Opera*, performed by his wife, Lotte Lenya, and also by Ute Lemper, Louis Armstrong, and Bobby Darin. . . . Wager with Mephistopheles and beware the witches on Walpurgis Night in *Faust*, Johann Wolfgang von Goethe's dramatic masterpiece, and read several of Goethe's poems. . . .

I READILY DISTINGUISH BETWEEN THE TWO QUESTIONS: WHETHER IT IS PRUDENT OR WHETHER IT IS RIGHT.

IMMANUEL KANT,
Fundamental Principles of the Metaphysic of Morals

Trumpets blare! How well I remember the day that I met Immanuel Kant. The teacher strode into the classroom purposefully, the intensity a departure from his carefree, sandal-clad, everyday entry. He paused, straightening his tie and organizing lecture notes, his manner paying tribute to the philosopher responsible for arguably the most famous moral theory in Western history. Kant the logician offers a framework for solving an ethical impasse with the precision of a calculator—his "categorical imperative"— a key that can unlock the deadbolt of indecision. References to the Kantian imperative persist in articles and broadcasts. Why all the fuss? Bet you never forget him.

Muddled

Why do we tie ourselves in knots when faced with thorny choices? Let's shadow Kant on his walkabout after lunch, his cane striking cobblestones at the same time every day, meticulous in his personal routine and his philosophical reasoning. He turns over three stones for us to retrieve, each one representing a major stumbling block in making sound decisions. The stones—labeled emotion, consequence, and selfishness—await our careful analysis. Let's examine each troublemaker.

Stone #1, emotion, guarantees missteps. Feelings of anger, envy, desire—arrogance, insecurity, and fear—all smother our reasoning capacity. Frenzy overrides thought. Passion garbles reflection. Maybe you know this person: Fired up, I can't cool down. A favorite student plagiarized. How dare she? I dined with her parents, after all. Known for my tough policies, I've never been so insulted. My colleagues and students gossip about this episode, betting on how I'll respond. Riled, with resentment brewing, I ignore a situation begging for a swift solution. Maybe I'll cancel the next class and buy some time . . . or give the entire group a failing grade for creating such a dishonest environment . . . or allow the plagiarist to write another paper . . . or ask an adminis-

trator to intervene . . . or quit. How humiliating. Besides, I'm very fond of the student. Don't give me advice. I just hope everyone will admire the position I take. Dang it! Yes, we recognize this teacher, unfortunately. Substitute any scenario and we can see ourselves, captured by emotion, incapable of action.

Stone #2, consequence, we all know well. Our absentminded professor's concern with others' reactions points out the confusion that results from a focus on consequences. Perhaps these imaginings sound familiar: Will I lose my job if I refuse to fudge on the expense account? How will family members react if I challenge my uncle's cruelty? If I tell the truth, it may cost me the relationship. If I keep quiet, I'll be part of the gang. Since no one knows I witnessed the accident, I walked away and avoided the hassle—but I'll come forward for a reward. The last time I challenged the coach's harsh discipline, I didn't play in the game. Questions of "if, then, and maybe" whip me around. Sometimes I even forget what the issue is, my thought process desperately in need of "mental discipline, let the consequence be what it may" (*Fundamental Principles*).

Stone #3, selfishness, weighs heavily in all my thinking, apparently. Selfishness churns up murky waters whenever the satisfaction of my needs determines my choice. This mindset, "liable to all sorts of corruption" (*Fundamental Principles*), is far from unique to me. Why not make friends with the wealthy bully if it snags me a club membership? (I don't approve of his behavior, of course.) I volunteer at the senior center because it beefs up my résumé. (You bet I would do it regardless.) I advise clients to take risks that aren't in their best interests, but I rely on those commissions. (Hey, they might get lucky.) Now, your turn with some examples!

My conscience burns. I'd like to wriggle out of this irksome feeling that I'm tackling choices all wrong. Kant pushes me to probe my unease, and a revelation slowly surfaces. Motivation matters. Yes. Motivation is *it*. *Why* do I tell the employer about the theft, or my partner about my change of heart? *What* spurs my decision to refuse to serve on that committee or to agree to participate in this protest? If I can overcome knee-jerk reactions, reason can purify my purpose. Yes, I know in my "pure heart" (*Fundamental Principles*) that what makes my choice a good one is that I plucked it from competing options simply because it was the right thing to do.

Obstacles abound as I set out to clean up my thinking. Even Kant admits that "a more or less refined self-love" (*Fundamental Principles*) may attach itself to all my actions. And, yes, powerful, very real emotions arrive that I can't pretend away. Yes, I'm a planner who automatically wonders what might happen. Squirming philosophers wax seats to a shine when grabbed by Kant's theory. They may not like it, but they want more. Figuring out the root of funky motivation bodes well for improvement. "I have contorted reality so that I can justify any decision. Why wouldn't I skip work occasionally since I'm the hardest worker?" "No excuse was too farfetched. I have a temper. I had a hard day. You've got all the luck." Peering into old, unattractive ways proves powerful incentive to put reason in charge.

DECISIVE

Kant presents his theory in two commanding statements. Let's get rational and watch his categorical imperative do its thing.

What does it mean for a standard to apply categorically? A prized answer from a college student, delivered in a guttural, soulful rhythm: "abbb-sooo-looooot-leeeeee." A child philosopher's explanation of an imperative: "gotta." That's it, exactly. Kant seeks reason-based obligation in decision making that applies to everyone for all time,

a universal standard. His imperative cancels out passions, consequences, and the "liberty of making an exception in our own favor" (*Fundamental Principles*). Elevating dilemmas into the realm of reason alone, I can aim unselfishly with a "good will" (*Fundamental Principles*) straight at the issue, knowing what I absolutely gotta do.

Time to unpack the first statement of the categorical imperative: "I am never to act otherwise than so that I could also will my action should become a universal law" (*Fundamental Principles*). What does *this* mean?! Around the dinner table, savvy interpretations aplenty: "My choice must be the one that I can ask of everyone. If I would not do it, no one should. If I do, you can." Another Kantian rewording: "I can't ask of you, of anyone, what I am unwilling to ask of myself. I'm not an exceptional case and don't deserve a pass—unless everyone does." And interestingly, "If more of us make reasonable decisions, then people might achieve better consensus on big issues. Each of us can rise above private, cultural, national interests, and think big." Our German boss would be pleased.

Ben's troubled face brings a smile to mine. His long legs are outstretched as he leans against a post outside the college bookstore. He is holding his calculus book, and I wrongly assume it's the source of his misery. Oblivious to hallway traffic, my usually easygoing student explains: "Mistakes were found in this edition of the text and the bookstore is offering a free replacement. But a friend from another college gave me the book so I didn't buy it here. Am I entitled to another copy? Can I say that anyone who possesses the book from whatever source . . . ?" I walk on. Ben sits. Kant heard in his classroom as I do in mine that the imperative asking for no exceptions is way too demanding. Think hard, he answers. I gave you the form your reasoning should take, but the job of deciding is yours. Ben is not alone, smarter yet perplexed, stumped but not really. Did he exchange the book?

Would you? (What about talking to the bookstore manager?)

Now for the unveiling of the second statement of the categorical imperative: "So act as to treat humanity, whether in thine own person or in that of any other, in every case as an end withal, never as a means only" (*Fundamental Principles*) What does *that* mean?! Kant recognizes that most of our daily interactions involve harmless "using" of others—shopper and grocer, student and teacher, neighbors, doubles partners, filmmaker and moviegoer. Human interaction relies on such give and take, willing exchanges of talents and services. Kant's command forbids the manipulative using of another *only* for my purposes, all take and no give. Dinner companions pass around perceptive examples: "I can't use a person like a pawn in a chess match. Helping you move *only* to secure a good recommendation?" "I'm suspicious of the delivery of flowers and an excuse at the same time." "Plotting a path to an inheritance by doing chores for my grandfather?" And a few great interpretations of "I can't let *myself* be used, either" include: by my spouse for my money, my girlfriend for my car, my alma mater for a donation. Kant concurs with diner's examples, his faith in reason and belief in human dignity confirmed.

This man of logic never receives a tepid response. I chuckle every time a former student exclaims, "You remember how I feel about Kant!" Frustration and respect, grimaces and nods of agreement trade places. Certain themes recur. Some resistant Kantians prefer to trust their gut level, passion-driven decisions. Others suspect that he surely considered consequence in his quest for universal obligation. "Aren't you forced to ask what if everyone made my choice, and isn't that forecasting the future?" Didn't visions of a run on the bookstore cause Ben's stalemate? And squawking voices compete for attention when contrasting Kant's goal of universal application with his claim that for females there would be "nothing of obliga-

tion or commands. . . . The fair sex" can't endure the "long-sustained reflection" (*Observations on the Feeling of the Beautiful and Sublime*) required of the categorical imperative. Bedlam! Further, philosophers of all ages point out that someone always feels used and gets hurt when a hard conflict is resolved. Such deep thinking seals his victory.

Kant succeeds in raising the stakes and the intellect. His theory forever tickles the back of the neck. Marsha put it well some twenty years after her first exposure: "I want a world in which everyone uses the imperative except me."

~~~~~~~~~~

AND YOUR TOPIC FOR DINNER CONVERSATION IS

"And although, no doubt, common men do not conceive it in such an abstract and universal form, yet they always have it really before their eyes and use it as the standard of their decision" (*Fundamental Principles*). Do you agree with Kant that ordinary folk (you and I) presume the categorical imperative and that it guides us, even if subconsciously, when faced with tough decisions? Are you concerned with purity of motive? Would you like to make dispassionate choices? Do you consider consequences? Give a specific example of a decision that pleases you in retrospect. How did you make up your mind in this case? What kinds of decisions do you regret? Why?

THE DOORBELL RINGS

Guests can look to Kant's Swiss neighbors for outstanding varieties of nutty-flavored cheeses, such as Gruyère or Comté, from which to choose and supply a variety of crackers and sliced apples. Partake in Oktoberfest with your diners' selections of German lager to accompany the grilled bratwurst, but keep in mind Kant's admonition that the foamy concoction rendered dinner companions "dreamy and withdrawn" (*Anthropology from a Pragmatic Point of View*). Despite his strong disapproval of "stupefying oneself by the excessive use of any food or drink" (*Anthropology*), Kant always drank wine at his own dinner parties in accordance with his belief that one's wit benefitted from the (slight) indulgence. A diner or two can bring a crisp riesling, a good wine to complement tonight's fare. For dessert maybe pick up a very sweet eiswein ("ice wine") made from grapes frozen on the vine.

Hips swivel as Nena releases "99 Red Balloons," paving the way for the arrival of the Bavarian Oktoberfest Band. Turn up their *Music of Oktoberfest* and take to the streets with Munich's partygoers. Ayo offers a gentle reminder, however, that "Life Is Real" and a decisive discussion awaits. Jazz guitarist Coco Schumann's rendition of "Autumn Leaves" switches the evening's tempo, gracefully setting a contemplative mood. Kant clears his throat.

German talent provides a lovely backdrop for your conversation. Julia Fischer, mother *and* music professor in Frankfurt, concert violinist *and* pianist, chose not to choose! On another evening, watch Fischer's one-of-its-kind performance of concertos by Saint-Saëns on violin and Grieg on piano. Tonight listen as her strings toast October with Respighi's "Poema autunnale." Next, Johannes Brahms's Violin Concerto in D Major and Robert Schumann's Fantasie in C Major come alive with violin virtuoso Anne-Sophie Mutter, and she gives your discussion a lift home. Moondog salutes *The German Years* and tonight's philosophizing, encouraging you (as he surely did) to "Do Your Thing" and listen out for the cry of a "Bird's Lament."

Since Kant began each day with a cup of weak black tea, raise a tiny teacup to the master of ceremonies. Maybe next October your group will meet in the town of Bad Münstereifel at Heino's Rathaus-Café. Could that be the host making music for lucky diners? He pays baritone tribute to the small, white, much-loved flower known in the Alpine region as "Edelweiβ." Sense Heino's love of traditional music (*volksmusik*) in *Edelweiss*. Before taking your leave, enjoy composer Richard Strauss's "Beim Schlafengehen." Ah, "Going to Sleep." Alternate between versions sung by sopranos Kiri Te Kanawa and Elisabeth Schwarzkopf. Strauss's music captures Herman Hesse's poignant words: "Brow, forget all your thinking" as you walk "into night's magic sphere."

In the Kitchen

BRATWURST WITH "SELF-MIXED" MUSTARD

"Now, then, gentlemen" (*Last Days of Immanuel Kant; and Other Writings*). With these words, the stern scholar concluded a day of writing and initiated his well-chosen guests' "stimulating play of thoughts" (*Anthropology*). At Kant's table, dinner music was a "tasteless absurdity," overindulgence a sign of moral failure, and "gossip" deemed "shallow and malicious" (*Anthropology*). Anchored by an unwavering regimen—three dishes, two bottles of wine, never more than eight guests, and self-mixed mustard — Kant's social engagements unfolded like clockwork. Slather a bit of the philosopher's favorite condiment on top of these bratwursts, perhaps adding an extra splash, as he believed mustard enhanced the power of memory.

"SELF-MIXED" MUSTARD

PREPARATION: 12 hours, 30 minutes (20 minutes active)

1 cup Colman's dry mustard (because this brand is not bitter)

1 cup apple cider vinegar

1 cup sugar

2–4 tablespoons honey

3 large egg yolks

1. Mix together the dry mustard, vinegar, sugar, and honey. Whisk in the egg yolks, one at a time, until thoroughly incorporated. Cover with cheesecloth or a kitchen towel and leave out, 12 hours or overnight, at room temperature.

2. Using a double boiler, or a metal pan in a saucepan of simmering water, cook the mixture, stirring constantly, until thickened, 5 to 10 minutes. Cool completely and store in the refrigerator.

BRATWURST

PREPARATION: 45 minutes (15 minutes active)

8 bratwursts (if using precooked, skip parboiling step)

2 tablespoons vegetable oil

1. Bring a large saucepan filled with water to a boil over high heat. Prick the bratwursts all over with a fork, add to the pan, and return the water to a boil. Immediately reduce the heat to low, and simmer, covered, for 18 to 20 minutes. Remove the bratwursts from the water and drain briefly on paper towels.

2. Heat a large, heavy-bottomed skillet over medium heat. Add the vegetable oil. When the oil is hot, add the bratwursts to the pan and sauté for 10 minutes, turning to brown the bratwursts evenly. (To achieve a charcoal flavor, grill the bratwursts, basting them with melted butter or oil several times during the process.)

3. Slice the bratwursts into generous pieces and serve with the homemade mustard.

CABBAGE SLAW WITH CARAWAY

Traditional Bavarian sauerkraut achieves its familiar, sour flavor through fermentation. In this fresh, unbrined version, shredded cabbage is combined with spicy radishes and coated with a tangy, mustard vinaigrette. Savoy—an attractive variety of cabbage with a compact head and crinkly leaves—has a milder flavor than standard pickling cabbages. Make your own aesthetic judgment about the variety of cabbage you prefer, adding quantities of radishes and modifying tastes and textures to suit.

PREPARATION: 45 minutes

1 teaspoon caraway seeds

8 cups finely sliced, cored Savoy cabbage (1¼ pounds)

1 large bunch radishes (6–8), cut into matchsticks or thinly sliced

2 Granny Smith apples, peeled, cored, and cut into matchsticks

2½ tablespoons apple cider vinegar

1 tablespoon Dijon mustard

2 tablespoons minced shallots

1 teaspoon kosher salt

½ teaspoon freshly ground pepper

½ cup extra virgin olive oil

1. Toast the caraway seeds in a small, dry skillet over medium-high heat for 1 to 2 minutes, until fragrant. Set aside to cool.

2. In a large serving bowl, combine the cabbage, radishes, and apples.

3. In a small bowl, mix together the vinegar, mustard, shallots, salt, and pepper. Slowly pour in the olive oil and whisk until blended.

4. Drizzle the dressing over the cabbage mixture, add the cooled caraway seeds, and toss before serving.

CHOCOLATE KIRSCH TORTE

Kant devised his multicourse meals to keep his guests together as long as possible. If your discussions remain lively, focused, never heated or self-righteous, you have created the ideal Kantian setting for philosophizing. Our exacting and, by all accounts, well dressed and witty host deemed his dinner parties successful *only* when they ended in "loud and good natured" (*Anthropology*) laughter. As your evening draws to a close, serve your (hopefully) lighthearted company a slice of chocolate torte flavored with German *kirschwasser*, or "cherry water."

PREPARATION: 2 hours, 45 minutes
(45 minutes active)

¾ cup (1½ sticks) unsalted butter, plus more for pan

9 ounces semi sweet or bittersweet chocolate, chopped

1¼ cups sugar

½ cup water

3 tablespoons kirsch, or pear-flavored or other clear, fruit-flavored brandy

5 large eggs

1 cup heavy cream

1. Preheat the oven to 300 degrees. Add 2 inches of water to a roasting pan that will accommodate a 9-inch springform or round cake pan. Adjust the water level, depending upon the size of your roasting pan, so that the water reaches halfway up the sides of the springform pan. Put the roasting pan in the oven to heat the water while you prepare the torte.

2. Butter the bottom and sides of a 9-inch springform or round cake pan. Line the bottom of the pan (whether springform or cake pan) with parchment paper cut into a circle. Butter the parchment. Wrap the outside of the springform pan with a double layer of 18-inch heavy-duty aluminum foil (to prevent water from leaking in).

3. In a large, metal bowl over a saucepan of simmering water, heat the butter and the chocolate, stirring occasionally, until almost completely melted. There should be a few chocolate pieces remaining. Remove from the stove and continue stirring until the mixture is completely smooth. Allow to cool.

4. In a small saucepan over medium heat, combine 1 cup of the sugar with ½ cup water and stir until the sugar is dissolved. Cool. Stir in 1½ tablespoons of the kirsch.

5. Add the sugar syrup to the chocolate mixture. Add the eggs, one at a time, whisking after each addition until well mixed.

6. Carefully pour the batter into the prepared pan and place the pan inside the roasting pan. Bake for 45 to 55 minutes, until a toothpick inserted into the torte's center comes out clean and the sides of the torte are just beginning to pull away from the pan. Oh so carefully remove the springform pan from the roasting pan. Let cool on a wire rack until completely cool, at least 1 hour. Just before serving, run a knife around the edge of the pan and either release the sides of the springform or invert the cake pan.

7. By hand (or with an electric mixer) beat the heavy cream with the remaining ¼ cup of sugar until thickened. Add the remaining 1½ tablespoons kirsch and beat until peaks form.

8. Serve the torte with a generous dollop of whipped cream.

GERMANY TO GO

Visit Berlin's Neue Nationalgalerie, designed by architect Ludwig Mies van der Rohe, inspect the works of Max Beckmann, and listen to anything sung by baritone Dietrich Fischer-Dieskau. . . . Fly on *Wings of Desire*, directed by Wim Wenders, join the crew in Wolfgang Petersen's *Das Boot*, and spy on *The Lives of Others* through the lens of director Florian Henckel von Donnersmarck. . . . Putt with golfer Martin Kaymer, take tips from soccer legend and U.S. World Cup coach Jurgen Klinsmann, trace Steffi Graf's tennis career, and go wild with discus thrower Robert Harting over his 2012 Olympic victory. . . . Imagine Kant's reaction as you read Thomas Mann's *Death in Venice* and listen to "It's a Man's Man's Man's World," re-invented by the Dresden Soul Symphony. . . . Read *The Tin Drum* by Günter Grass and Herta Müller's *The Hunter Angel*. . . . Dance the Landler in three-quarter time, hang out with John Prine as he sings of *German Afternoons*, and attend a performance of Beethoven's only opera, *Fidelio*. . . .

RESOURCES

PHILOSOPHY

Fundamental Principles of the Metaphysic of Morals by Immanuel Kant, translated by Thomas K. Abbott.

Observations on the Feeling of the Beautiful and Sublime by Immanuel Kant, translated by John T. Goldthwait.

MUSIC

99 Luftballons by Nena: "99 Red Balloons."

Music of Oktoberfest by the Bavarian Oktoberfest Band and Chorus.

Joyful by Ayo: "Life Is Real."

Coco Now! by Coco Schumann: "Autumn Leaves."

Saint-Saëns Violin Concerto no. 3 / Grieg Piano Concerto, Julia Fischer, violin and piano, directed by Andreas Morell (2010) (DVD).

Poème by Ottorino Respighi, Julia Fischer, violin; Monte-Carlo Philharmonic Orchestra, Yakov Kreizburg, conducting: "Poema autunnale."

Brahms Violin Concerto in D Major, Op. 77 / Schumann Fantasie for Violin and Orchestra in C Major, Op. 131: Anne-Sophie Mutter, violin, with the New York Philharmonic Orchestra, Kurt Masur, conducting.

Moondog: The German Years, 1977–1999 by Moondog: "Do Your Thing," "Bird's Lament."

Edelweiss by Heino: "Edelweiβ."

Strauss: Four Last Songs / Orchestra Songs by Richard Strauss, Kiri Te Kanawa, soprano, with the London Symphony Orchestra, Andrew Davis, conducting: "Beim Schlafengehen."

Strauss: Four Last Songs / 12 Orchestral Songs by Richard Strauss, Elisabeth Schwarzkopf, soprano, with the Berlin Radio Symphony Orchestra, Robert Heger, conducting; London Symphony Orchestra, George Szell, conducting: "Beim Schlafengehen."

FOOD

Last Days of Immanuel Kant; and Other Writings by Thomas De Quincey.

Anthropology from a Pragmatic Point of View by Immanuel Kant, edited by Robert B. Louden.

Kant: A Biography by Manfred Kuehn.

The Sciences in Enlightened Europe, edited by William Clark, Jan Golinski, and Simon Schaffer.

A Slow Dance with Nature

November in China

Let me introduce you to my grandmother. Born in 1904, Nellie Eliza Williamson proved a master in adapting to change. Her father was a railroad man and on the go much of the time, so after her beloved mother's death she was thrust into unexpected maturity as a teen, taking upon herself the daunting task of rearing her four younger siblings. A young single mother in her twenties, caring for two daughters in the throes of the Depression, Nellie supported her family as a massage therapist known to her clients as Hilda Swenson (surely of Swedish origin!). Hoisting a massage table up three and four flights of stairs by day, she came home to prepare delicious meals and fill canning jars with succotash and watermelon pickles to line the pantry for winter evenings. Though pennies were scarce in 1931, she took out a life insurance policy that named her girls as beneficiaries, setting aside eleven cents a month to pay the premium. As a grandmother, she proudly answered to the sound of my first attempts to greet her—"Plum"—and she would be known to all by that name for the rest of her life.

After the death of her second husband, this owner of a sixth-grade education earned her real estate license. In her eightieth year, she left the hospital as the oldest person to undergo heart bypass surgery. Upon finding a pair of high-heeled shoes that she admired, she ordered four additional pairs in different colors. She was eighty-five. She visited my college classroom in high style and heels a year later. Plum drove to the nursing home to deliver three home-cooked meals a day to her first husband, with whom she maintained a friendship, rode motor scooters and went tubing downriver with grandchildren, and planted potatoes and made pies with great-grandchildren. Gradually losing her independence at ninety-two, she gave up her cherished driver's license and moved for the last time to live with my mother. She defeated all comers in Scrabble, showcasing the ability that characterized her long life, somehow crafting a word from random letters and making the best possible move. At ninety-five, she knew when she was done, accepting the biggest change of all in her distinctive way.

Nellie/Hilda/Plum was a rock star of reinvention. Though she never balked at meeting life's insistent demand for alteration, she of course at times wished for an easier path. The basic human aversion to change interests philosophers in all times and places. Healthy living demands that we make friends with change, however, and gain the upper hand on this elemental fear.

Students of philosophy, opening their minds and hearts to new ideas, quite often recognize the wisdom of personal change. Some welcome the chance for a clean start on their lives while others turn away from their discomfiting insights. In philosophy circles and around dinner tables, I listen to stories of coping with forced readjustment due to these troubled economic times—a sudden move, unexpected unemployment, picking up new skills in a hurry, plans for college or starting a new business derailed. Change is here to stay. Uncertainty is a sure thing. Funny-sounding sentences! But we must absorb this reality so that we can live contentedly, accepting life on its condition of constant newness. If we count on change, we will be less surprised when it comes and therefore more capable of dealing with it, gifted in handling difficulty and winning joy.

With but a quick glance around me, I see lives, improved by taking a chance on change, shine. "It was time," says my tearful/glad friend upon leaving her hometown and close-knit social circle to live closer to her children. How unlike the teacher, too afraid of what retirement might bring, who desperately clings to a job gone stale. An athlete suffers an injury that prevents his return to the field as a player and now, with no trace of self-pity, paces the sidelines as coach of a youth league team. A woman living from paycheck to paycheck gives notice and bravely walks away from an unsavory workplace environment—although her new job pays less, she knows firsthand that her work matters, and conspires to patch together part-time work to balance the checkbook. Might some stay in sickening work environments *only* because payday is predictable? "Why That D Minus Was the Best Grade I Ever Received" remains the title of one of my favorite student papers. Rather than finding fault with the instructor's rigorous standards, this upset but savvy student used her failing grade to call "time out" and take stock of her life. Rearranging her priorities, dropping some commitments to better honor others, she thrilled herself with an A for the class (no longer standing for "anxiety").

What about giving newness a kiss? Every day smacks of freshness—you bring new people into your life, travel to places near or far for the first time, cook okra, volunteer, square dance, all the while wearing creativity and spontaneity just as comfortably as old clothes. You never know. And what if you did? Really, what if you *did* know what lay ahead? Can you imagine *that* life?

I know this. Not long ago, my cousin and I gazed at the ocean on a cool spring evening on the Outer Banks of North Carolina.

Our observation perch was the deck of a very local restaurant as we waited for our takeout order. The busy bartender/server/greeter seemed so at home, so in his element, that I asked him if he were a native. His smiling response stays with me: "Of the planet? Yes." He was born and still lived in a tiny coastal town, and that town, just like every town, is located on his Home: Planet Earth. *All* is native here. *All* is in flux. What if we felt that sense of belonging, of flowing kinship with swaying sea oats and diving gulls, in our bones? How would we live then? Looking at the ocean, always on the move yet still one body of water, I wonder . . . can I live that way? What about rolling with life's tide? And rolling. . . .

Yes, giving up the doomed quest for permanence, I stretch with limber limbs and flexing mind and fall into my life, entering the heart of this uncertain, uncontrollable universe. Aware that I control only my responses to whatever each day brings, I submit to all that is unknown, no guarantees. If evolving—moving—is the natural way of the world, then I will shift and shape, too.

Simple words softly spoken in ancient China reassure and excite. If we accept change as a given, then the world is ours for the taking. Lao Tzu (lau-DZU) twirls to nature's neverending dance. Let's catch the beat, get in the groove, and tap our way home.

PREPPING FOR CHINA

Treat yourself to Ang Lee's film *Crouching Tiger, Hidden Dragon*, Zhang Yimou's *To Live* and *Raise the Red Lantern*, and discover the landscape of *Wild China* in the BBC documentary. . . . Read humanitarian Xinran's *Message from an Unknown Chinese Mother* and trace the journey of Nobel Peace Prize–winner Liu Xiaobo. . . . Behold millions of porcelain sunflower seeds exhibited by maverick artist Ai Weiwei and watch Alison Klayman's documentary *Ai Weiwei: Never*

Sorry, then track down rebellious blogger and racecar driver Han Han. . . . Move your stone strategically in a game of Go, volley with French Open champion Li Na, but think twice about shooting hoops with Yao Ming and Ye Li or climbing over the Great Wall of China. . . . Spend "Tuesdays in Chinatown" with vocalist Andy Bey and look for figure skater Vera Wang's latest fashion statement. . . . Salute the Terra-Cotta Army in the city of Xi'an, home to one of the world's oldest civilizations located in the Yellow River Valley. . . .

REALIZE THAT ALL THINGS CHANGE.

LAO TZU,
Tao Te Ching

"Finally!" exclaimed a delighted fourth grader. "I've found the philosopher who thinks just like me." An ordinary man doing nothing special some twenty-six hundred years ago, Lao Tzu continues to work his subtle magic on countless thinkers worldwide. His eighty-one short verses in the *Tao Te Ching* (dow-de-zhing) loosen tight shoulders and lighten steps. If we absorb his uncomplicated message, perhaps we will no longer "prefer the side paths" (*Tao Te Ching*) but instead take the most direct routes with no sharp turns. Lao Tzu's lessons, "straightforward, but supple" (*Tao Te Ching*), shape to the contours of any life they touch.

RESIST

Change vexes us from the start. Children beg Time to halt for birthdays, for a game threatened by darkness, and for the aging uncle who no longer welcomes a ride on his shoulders. Change arrives with each tick of the clock nonetheless, and we can't make the moments stay. As we're swept up in a twirling world, our craving for permanence increases with age. The urge to keep things just as they are competes with the urge for adventure. Defiantly applying wrinkle-erasing creams, pounding aching joints in the pursuit of youthful pastimes, hiding one's date of birth from kids and coworkers in words and in jeans—we trick ourselves. (Almost.)

An automatic defense against the inevitability of change sneaks up on us. We chafe against life's shifting grain, holding tight to the way things (maybe) were: My kids will attend my alma mater or I'll not put a penny toward their tuition. No! I just read that my university now accepts women so cancel my annual gift. Who reads Spanish street signs? Look at his baggy shorts and her head scarf. My old friends have all these newfangled ideas and we have nothing in common. Yoga and carpooling, civil unions and naturalization ceremonies, a world "filled with infinite possibilities" (*Tao Te Ching*). What? Batten the hatches! (By the way, I never go to funerals. Never will.)

Maximum effort goes toward maintaining sameness. No way will I "stop trying to control and let go of fixed plans and concepts" (*Tao Te Ching*). Brittle and hardening fast, ignoring even the faintest stirrings of desire for change, I turn off my life. Regrettably my habitual rejection of going with life's flow and adapting to "events as they come" (*Tao Te Ching*) proves disastrous when difficulty arrives. Life-threatening diseases shatter, love dies, thieves steal, funding disappears, storms down trees, floods uproot homes, and failures multiply. None of these realities can be pretended away, and being unskilled at changing in even the smallest way, I am ill-equipped to deal with hard times. A lifetime of butting heads with uncontrollable events, swimming against any current that challenges me, leaves me worn out. I'm not myself (I hope). What to do? How to change?

As if stuck in the snow, spinning my wheels into deepening ruts, I can't get going. I ring a popular number for roadside assistance, marveling at the effortless style of my Chinese tow-truck operator. How interesting Lao Tzu's approach. He steps back and observes the car from all sides. Diligently he checks the road in all directions, searching for any obstacles. He scratches his chin. He does nothing. After staring at a stretch of freshly fallen snow, he makes his move. Sliding into the car, he slowly turns the wheels toward the unmarked snow and the car eases forward, making new tracks without resistance, "fluid as melting snow" (*Tao Te Ching*). Incredible! Lao Tzu took charge by going with the circumstances given. Oh, how I would like the same gentle approach for gaining traction in my everyday life, dealing with every situation as gracefully as he steered the gliding car. If I give in to *anything*, a canceled flight or a puppy's arrival, and become a part of it, I wager that the wisest actions will unfold. How could I forget that "knowing how to yield is strength" (*Tao Te Ching*)? Bodysurfing with the waves or floating on my back, I experienced this

blending of me with life as a child. Riding a two-wheeler the first time without adult support, I counted on my balance and the bike. "Humility means trusting" (*Tao Te Ching*). I think this just might work. Like my first gallop on horseback, I'll let go, finally relaxing the reins and letting the mare carry me. Wheee!

What is it, exactly, that Lao Tzu perceived about the world? What motivated his faith in surrender? While one's intellect can barely graze his vision, intuition at times can capture it in a flash. Here's my stab at finding words that strike close to intuition's experience: *All* life rests and moves in one flow of energy. The Tao, this eternal and unalterable force, runs through everything with a thrumming, steady rhythm. Here, within the unchanging flow, lies permanence. Movement provides the safety net from the freefall of change. Rocking in the cradle of constant movement, I uncover my true nature as a part of Life's unfailing heartbeat. Balanced and swinging back and forth on Nature's pendulum, my energy feeds on unlimited Energy. Buoyed by this rhythmic compatibility, I change and renew, moment to moment.

Child philosophers merrily slap their thighs in agreement with Lao Tzu's way. "I bet he made up that saying 'any place I hang my hat is home.'" "This whole earth is spinning. No wonder I can't sit still!" "Change is like your shadow that's always there and *everybody* knows you can't run faster than your shadow. Don't they?"

Don't we?

EMBRACE

Though "true words seem paradoxical . . . this loftiness has roots that go deep for those who put it into practice" (*Tao Te Ching*). Let's walk and see for ourselves. . . .

Lao Tzu's down-to-earth truths take firm hold as we stroll in the countryside. Led by a trotting dog, we set out, following Mel's surefooted lead. Though the years have snatched his vision, Mel traces familiar terrain for miles, using fence, rock, and creek as landmarks, bounding without limitation. His life serves as a perfect lesson in seamlessly transitioning through change. A sprightly and playful pup . . . a strong, never-tiring runner . . . a lounging companion up for the occasional leisurely romp . . . slipping into senior status, all done without a break in stride. He picks up the hawk's flight before we do. The bird soars and dips with starched wings that flap only as needed to catch the breeze. Clouds assume bold definition and in moments the crisp image dissolves. The lake's repetitive lapping draws us to its bank, where we sit on a rotting log that also supports blooming wildflowers. How different the trees that line our path look this spring, winter's bare branches now popping with buds, autumn's crunchy leaves replaced underfoot by tender shoots of grass. We have ambled along this route for years, and though everything changes with the seasons and in our lives, it is the same journey. We move with change in one world. The truth about Life reveals itself amidst elm and egret. I am filled by the same energy that supplies dog, cloud, and lake. Despite difficulty, struggle is not necessary. Like the hawk, I can align myself with the wind at my back. "If you accept the world / you will return to your primal self" (*Tao Te Ching*). Home at last, the real me in the real world.

A favorite memory from childhood comes to mind. Winners of the annual raw egg contest (every year!) at field day, my father and I tossed the delicate oval ever so carefully as the distance between us grew— we shared a secret game plan. Softening hands sweeping backward with the egg's arrival, we let its force gently subside into yielding, nestling hand baskets "Receptive as a valley" (*Tao Te Ching*), hands go as egg goes—I go as life goes. That's the way. Despair and joy, success and failure, hard work and all play, laughter and tears, easy and

hard, loyalty and betrayal, fatigue and strength, fear and courage, I'll change partners just as gracefully as night and day switch places. Life presents itself and I go to meet it. "I wait for the alabaster to make its design known to me," a sculptor explains to admirers of "her" creations. "I never set out with a shape in mind." Like the sculptor, "patient, according with the way things are" (*Tao Te Ching*), I slide along as options appear and space for my entry opens. The worry of "What if?" no longer obsesses me. Knowing to ask "What else?" evokes my smile.

Inseparable, change and time seesaw together. Stepping out on the dance floor, whether we break-dance or ballroom, tango or twist, the dance is all. "Can you deal with the most vital matters / by letting events take their course" (*Tao Te Ching*)? Yes. Caregivers of aging parents seize this unique responsibility and trade yesteryear's roles. Parents of an autistic child gingerly guide their son through tortuous years, always

best environment for him at
t, their efforts sealed in his
life. Children grieving along
with their surviving parent heighten their
concern for one another, taking joyful ad-
vantage of new/old relationships that would
not have been forged otherwise. An architect in failing health excitedly sketches a
garden bench on a cocktail napkin, trading
death for life. Look at the world! A team of
Rwandan cyclists gains international re-
nown, Tutsis and Hutus riding side by side,
setting aside a history of genocide and ethnic conflict to write a new story. Just months
after the 2011 earthquake and tsunami
ripped through their country and the home-
towns of many players, Japan's women's
soccer team won the World Cup against
very tall odds, their team's spirit giving
heart to delighted compatriots.

Is *embrace* of change asking too much? Is
this word too strong, since change delivers
heartache as well as bliss? I don't think so.
Picture a cat spooning himself into the
crook of your elbow, cuddled within its
curve for support, "supple like a tree in the
wind" (*Tao Te Ching*). Imagine a hug so tight
that your limbs enfold a crying child "firm
like a mountain" (*Tao Te Ching*).

Yes, "supple and firm" for a lifelong, slow
dance with nature, ready with a swooping
embrace to "receive the world in your arms"
(*Tao Te Ching*).

～～～～～～～～～～

AND YOUR TOPIC FOR DINNER CONVERSATION IS

"Whoever is soft and yielding is a dis-
ciple of life" (*Tao Te Ching*). As a "dis-
ciple of life," can you bend and twist
with the certainty of change? Will your
life become easier as you make friends
with uncertainty? Describe the benefits
of moving *with* life, entering *into* each
day, come what may. What is the alternative? Give specific examples both of
resisting and embracing change.

～～～～～～～～～～

The Doorbell Rings

Each guest brings a particular vegetable—already sliced—ripe for the season, having been given clear guidelines by the host for preparing vegetables for stir-fry. (Prior considerations of the hard, medium, and soft distinctions spelled out in the recipe will lead the host in making assignments.) Diners can also contribute appetizer selections purchased from a Chinese restaurant, the rice that accompanies the stir-fry, and samples of easily-found Chinese rice beer. For dessert, dwelling "on the fruit and not the flower" (*Tao Te Ching*), sliced Asian pears hit the spot. Similar to apples in shape and texture, this variety fully ripens on the tree, ready to eat at harvest.

Begin your "Harvest Celebration" with Anna Guo's traditional hammered dulcimer (*yangquin*) serenade. Hear the crisp sound of "Pearls Dropping onto the Jade Plate." Following her lead and also calling Shanghai home, Coco Zhao's piano and vocals give new life to Chinese jazz. Share his joy in "Full Moon, Blooming Flowers." Welcome an introduction to the Chinese lute (*pipa*) from composer and virtuoso Wu Man. Her *Immeasurable Light* surprises on every track, especially the whirl of "Leaves Flying in Autumn" on thrumming fingertips, inviting you into your discussion.

Slowing down for your dance with Lao Tzu, enter "Through the Bamboo Forest" to the tune of Yo-Yo Ma's cello solos which grace Tan Dun's soundtrack in *Crouching Tiger, Hidden Dragon*. Saunter along Ma's "Silk Road." Walk in a new direction as pianist Xiayin Wang takes you down the "Promenade" with your "Lean Kat Stride." Let her warm "Winter Solstice" cushion your conversation. Pass a small plate to master chef and musician Guo Yue as he serves up *Music, Food & Love* on bamboo flute (*dizi*) and reed pipe (*bawu*). Picture him shopping for one of his very popular cooking classes and playing his instrumental ode to change, "The Little Bird Must Fly," for his dinner guests. The feathery touch of Lang Lang's fingers on piano in "Autumn Moon on a Calm Lake" complements Lao Tzu's vision. Linger over his *Dragon Songs* with China's ambassador of music.

Sip herbal tea made from chrysanthemum flowers, which bloom in late fall and early winter, long after other flowers have faded away. Before the rustlings of relaxed departures begin, choose any of the *Oper-atic Arias* performed by Beijing's Hao Jiang Tian, a fixture at the Metropolitan Opera in New York for two decades. Yo-Yo Ma and Bobby McFerrin "hold nothing back" (*Tao Te Ching*), and for both musicians the improvisation "flows from the core of his being" (*Tao Te Ching*). Give and take, playful and earnest, walk with them into the night's rarefied "Air," their cello and jazz creations topping off your evening. Shhhh. "Hush Little Baby."

SHRIMP DUMPLINGS WITH DIPPING SAUCE

Flexing your cooking mind, forget all notions of uniformity in the task of dumpling making, knowing that "It is the space within that makes it useful" (*Tao Te Ching*). Basic ratios of filling-to-wrapper should be followed, but the dumpling's final form will reveal itself. Although this recipe gives directions for creating pouch-shaped dumplings, your group may prefer pleated crescents, half moons, or triangles.

SHRIMP DUMPLINGS

PREPARATION: 1 hour, 45 minutes (1 hour active)

2 tablespoons beaten egg white

1 tablespoon cornstarch

½ teaspoon rice wine or dry sherry

1 pound completely shelled, deveined raw shrimp, thoroughly drained of any excess water

2 tablespoons low-sodium soy sauce

2 teaspoons Asian sesame oil

1 tablespoon dry sherry

¼ teaspoon salt

1 teaspoon sugar

1 cup shredded Napa cabbage, plus additional leaves for lining steamer basket

2 scallions, minced

1 tablespoon finely minced, peeled fresh ginger

1 12-ounce package wonton wrappers

1. To make the filling, place the egg white in a large bowl, add the cornstarch and rice wine, and stir until the cornstarch is dissolved. Add the shrimp and toss to coat. Refrigerate for 30 minutes.

2. In a food processor, process half of the shrimp mixture, the soy sauce, sesame oil, sherry, salt, and sugar until finely minced. Add the Napa cabbage, scallions, and ginger, and process until combined. Add the remaining shrimp and pulse for 2 to 3 seconds at a time, until the shrimp is just barely chopped. The filling can be made ahead and refrigerated for several hours.

3. Place ½ tablespoon of filling in the center of a wonton wrapper. Gather one edge of the wrapper and pleat and pinch your way around the wrapper's edge to form a pouch shape. Keep the unused wrappers and assembled dumplings covered with plastic wrap as you work. Repeat with the remainder of the filling.

4. Place a steamer basket in a pot of corresponding size and add water until the level is just below the bottom of the steamer basket. Line the basket with extra cabbage leaves (or use parchment paper with holes punched in it) to prevent the dumplings from sticking. Bring the water to a boil. Add as many dumplings as the basket can accommodate, making sure they do not touch one another. Reduce the heat to medium-low, cover the pot, and steam for 10 to 12 minutes. Repeat with the remaining dumplings, replacing the cabbage leaves between batches as necessary.

Dipping Sauce

PREPARATION: 15 minutes

⅓ cup soy sauce

2 tablespoons unseasoned rice vinegar

1 tablespoon sugar

2 teaspoons Asian sesame oil

¼ teaspoon chili oil or dried red pepper flakes

1. In a small saucepan, bring the soy sauce, vinegar, and sugar to a boil. Stir until the sugar dissolves. Cool slightly, then pour into a serving bowl. Add the sesame and chili oils and stir until blended.

LATE HARVEST STIR-FRY

Celebrate the last breath of fall with a free-wheeling late harvest stir-fry that can be adapted to suit your guest list, whim, or geographic location. Like market-driven chefs, your guests can find inspiration in the varying selections at local farm stands and gather a harvest bounty for your stir-fry that honors the change of seasons. Have all the vegetables washed, thoroughly dried, sliced, and categorized by density before you begin to heat your wok or skillet. Be prepared to respond to shifting conditions as you work—adjust your recipe to account for the heat output of your stove, size of your pan, and moisture accumulation in the pan. As you toss the multicolored array of finely sliced vegetables against the hot metal surface . . . watch! If you are unfamiliar with stir-fry technique, you may want to refer to Grace Young's engaging, step-by-step narrative (*Stir-frying to the Sky's Edge*) of this ancient cooking method *before* tackling this recipe.

PREPARATION: 1 hour

¼ cup low-sodium chicken broth

2 tablespoons rice wine or dry sherry

3 tablespoons soy sauce

1 tablespoon cornstarch

1 tablespoon cold water

2 tablespoons peanut or canola oil, plus additional as necessary

4 scallions, cut into thin, 2-inch long strips

2 tablespoons minced, peeled fresh ginger

1 tablespoon minced garlic

½ teaspoon dried red pepper flakes

3 cups hard vegetables (carrots, broccoli, cauliflower, etc.), thinly sliced (¼ inch thick) and thoroughly dried

4 cups medium vegetables (green beans, bell peppers, eggplants, sugar snap peas, snow peas, bok choy, mushrooms, etc.), thinly sliced (¼ inch thick) and thoroughly dried

3 cups soft vegetables (spinach, Chinese cabbage, bean sprouts, etc.), thinly sliced (¼ inch thick) and thoroughly dried

2 cups uncooked jasmine or basmati-style rice, prepared according to package instructions

1. Mix the broth, rice wine, and soy sauce in a small bowl and set aside. In a separate bowl, whisk the cornstarch with 1 table-spoon cold water until completely dissolved. Set aside.

2. Heat a wok over high heat until hot enough to evaporate a droplet or two of water upon contact. If you do not have a wok, you may use a 12-inch stainless-steel skillet, but be careful not to overcrowd the pan, and monitor it for any moisture accumulation—a sign that your pan is not hot enough. If you find the wok becomes too dry at any time during cooking, add additional oil, 1 tablespoon at a time, by pouring it down the sides of the wok.

3. Add 1 tablespoon of the oil and swirl to coat the sides of the wok. Add the scallions, ginger, garlic, and pepper flakes and toss briefly, until fragrant.

4. Add the hard vegetables and toss for 4 minutes. Remove and set aside. Swirl the remaining tablespoon of oil in the wok and when hot, add the medium vegetables and toss for 2 minutes. Add the soft vegetables and cook for another 2 minutes. Return the hard vegetables to the wok. Make a small well in the middle of the vegetables by pushing them up the sides of the wok. Slowly pour in the broth mixture, using only enough to coat your vegetables and not so much that you extinguish the high heat in the wok and cause the vegetables to begin to steam. You may or may not need to use all of the

broth mixture, depending upon the type and quantities of vegetables. Add the cornstarch mixture and quickly toss to coat.

5. Serve with the prepared rice.

CHINA TO GO

Listen to composer Horatiu Radulescu's *Lao Tzu Sonatas* as you read the timeworn poetry of Han-Shan, Li Po, and Tu Fu, complemented by challenges from modern "Misty Poets" Bei Dao, Shu Ting, and Ai Qing. . . . Ride a rickshaw through narrow alleys (*hutongs*) in old Beijing, explore the Forbidden City, behold the architectural triumph of the "Bird's Nest" stadium, and soak up the city's rich history as you remember 1989 with a long look at Tiananmen Square. . . . Flex as you practice the gentle moves of Tai Chi or vigorous thrusts of Qigong. . . . Float down the Yangtze River with stops in the mountain city Chongqing and beautiful Qutang Gorge . . . Grow up with Tietou in director Tian Zhuangzhuang's *The Blue Kite* and, after reading Li Cunxin's memoir, *Mao's Last Dancer*, watch his dream come true in the film directed by Bruce Beresford: . . . Read a Lisa See novel, admire swimmer Ye Shiwen's speed and grace, and light a lantern at The Moon Festival, marking harvest's end. . . .

RESOURCES

PHILOSOPHY

Tao Te Ching by Lao Tzu, presented by Stephen Mitchell.

MUSIC

Chinese Traditional Yang-Qin Music by Anna Guo: "Harvest Celebration," "Pearls Dropping onto the Jade Plate."

Dream Situation by Coco Zhao: "Full Moon, Blooming Flowers."

Immeasurable Light by Wu Man: "Leaves Flying in Autumn."

Crouching Tiger, Hidden Dragon by Tan Dun, Yo-Yo Ma, cello: "Through the Bamboo Forest," "Silk Road."

Danielpour: The Enchanted Garden—Preludes, Book 1 & 2 by Richard Danielpour, Xiayin Wang, piano: "Promenade," "Lean Kat Stride," "Winter Solstice."

Music, Food and Love by Guo Yue: "The Little Bird Must Fly."

Dragon Songs by Lang Lang: "Autumn Moon on a Calm Lake."

Operatic Arias: Verdi, Rossini, Bellini, Gounod: Hao Jiang Tian, bass, Slovak Radio Symphony Orchestra, Alexander Rahbari, conducting.

Yo-Yo Ma & Bobby McFerrin: Hush: Yo-Yo Ma, cello, and Bobby McFerrin, vocals: Air from Orchestral Suite no. 3, "Hush Little Baby."

FOOD

Stir-frying to the Sky's Edge: The Ultimate Guide to Mastery, with Authentic Recipes and Stories by Grace Young.

The Food of China by E. N. Anderson.

Dare You

DECEMBER IN FRANCE

Eyes lit up as friends learned about the topics in this book, many asking immediately if there would be a chapter on "I don't know what to call it, exactly. Please talk about . . . you know." They grinned. Yes, I did know. "Daring?"

"That's it!" they enthused. The following saga is it, I'd say. All aboard! Letty and Mac set sail from New York to Germany and the start of their almost four-month journey. Leaving Dresden's Der Zwinger, they make youth hostels home while visiting the Czech Republic and Poland. After overnights in the cities of Vilnius, Riga, and Tallinn, in the Baltic states, they hop on board the Trans-Mongolian Railway. Brushing up on French to prep for this ten-day journey, our travelers giggle at the sounds of German, mistaken about the language spoken by their tour guides and companions. Never mind! Russian Siberia comes alive with an accordion-accompanied picnic on Lake Baikal. Mongolian *yurts* and folklore amaze. They arrive at China's border for a six-week stay, touring by boat and bus, dining on unknown food, mixing with school children in Jingzhou. Hard-to-get visas in hand, their forty-eight-hour train ride to Tibet bumps and chugs out of Shanghai. Who cares that their six-bunk compartment lacks ladders and bed rails but comes equipped with cabinmates rotating above and below our duo's middle perches? After spending five days in Lhasa, they fly into Hong Kong, soon to wend their way home. The only passengers on a cargo-laden freighter, their places at the captain's table are secured for the two-week ocean journey. Coming ashore in Long Beach, California, they return to Virginia by cross-country train.

The intrepid travelers didn't use oxygen pillows offered at their Tibetan hotel, but big-eyed listeners lose their breath while absorbing this adventure. The most startling details, however, rarely get a mention. Mac's medical supplies filled half of one suitcase— the insulin for his type 1 diabetes, which required overnight refrigeration, toted in his backpack. "My hearing is so poor that it didn't matter *what* language was spoken on the Trans-Mongolian!" he laughs with his interpreter wife. Letty and Mac are seventy-two years old.

Pass the zest, please! Here's the spirit we crave, seduced by life, robust in response to opportunity, daring to try something new (or old!). Yes, here's that chapter for all those who long to plunge into the future, preserving freedom, expanding mind and heart.

My college students are themselves studies in bravado. Coming up the long hill, finding their way around, enrolling for first-time classes—all take nerve. Some left formal education behind years ago, perhaps defeated due to lack of requisite skills or pulled away by urgent responsibilities. Homeschoolers enter buildings overflowing with their first classmates. Unemployment forces others into uncharted territory, where they are determined to overcome any obstacle and master formidable but necessary technology. Most students manage school and jobs, and many include parenting and elder care in their juggling acts. I am inspired by their passion and unassuming feats of derring-do. What a kick when former students reappear. A young man in old boots arranges photos on my desk. After our reading of Zen Master Bashō's travel diary, he saved enough money to finance a trip on which he traced the poet's footsteps and re-created his seventeenth-century Japanese world. One returnee heads an internationally popular band while another lives as a shepherdess in a small Italian village. Thrilling: women in the corporate world, men with daycare positions, nonprofit and vineyard startups, doctorates and culinary certificates. . . .

Diners confirm my students' acute awareness that often the most daring venture of all is the voyage to self-discovery. Leo dared tell of his trip within. "I didn't want to live a half life. I was driven and desperate, craving praise and acceptance, motivated only by bogus notions of success and rank insecurities. I fell apart when I received a less than flattering appraisal of my dissertation, hit bottom, and though frightened, scrambled toward honest living. I sought help, still do. It's been fifteen years

and the effort continues to meet my dark places head on." Smiling, Leo choreographed his inner adventure with his hand—both his life and his hand slowly ascending, hitting plateaus, quavering at impasses, climbing up again. Charles's artistic approach to carpentry smacks of similar inward exploration. "I run after my intuition as fast as I can. I trust in the result because the spontaneous process of crafting the bench or fence, railing or statue, gives me a rush. I can't imagine creating with the end already decided. It's a trip. I drive myself crazy happy."

Around the table we go. Some recall the brio of youthful daring. Leaving home at seventeen, Red traveled from Miami to Berkeley to live (uninvited) with her true love. Though this caper disappointed, it was the beginning of Red's life of bold. Harrison said yes to courage by saying no to a college fraternity. Two lifetime musicians with "real" daytime jobs trade stories. Guitarist Jonathan seeks encouragement from his dad, nervous at taking the stage for his first acoustic solo show at age fifty. Nan quits dallying, refurbishing her rusty fiddle, learning piano, waking up with a song in her head and rushing to write it down, bracing herself for the challenge of a public performance. "I tend to make things very big and scare myself. I'm done with boring excuses." An educator's position eliminated after twenty-five years, she attacks her interview phobia after a first failure and gets the job next go-round. A college graduate, tickled and grimy, tunes out disapproval and assembles tools for his dream job as a self-employed mechanic. I take my turn, gladdened by the memory of a childhood pickup baseball game in which my pal Henry's reliably errant arm winged a ball through a neighbor's window. When gruff Mr. Pasco confronted our group and demanded that the villain step forward, mute bodies froze. Finally I announced, "I did it," so the game could go on. The daring move, it became quite clear, was my follow-up request. "Mr. Pasco, can we please have our ball back now?" Oops.

Why do we love talk of dashing romps and hard-earned victories? We know too well that the habit of resignation is an easy one to acquire. When life deals hard-to-play cards, we often fold our hands. Choosing to play the victim, we refuse life's invitations. We lie low and give up.

Ooh-la-la! A vivacious Parisian woman made reservations for our group at a favorite café. Simone de Beauvoir (see-Mone duh boh-VWAHR) rifles the ball right through the window of complacency, springs open negativity's trapdoor, and sets "hands free and ready to stretch out toward a new future" (*The Ethics of Ambiguity*). It's never too late.

PREPPING FOR FRANCE

Ah, Paris: Climb atop Montmartre for a rest in the Basilica of Sacré-Coeur and gaze down upon the city at sunset, tunnel through the catacombs, catch a spark from the stained glass of Sainte-Chapelle, and stroll along the Avenue des Champs-Élysées to spot the yellow jersey worn by the winning cyclist of the Tour de France. . . . Find your artistic treasure in the Louvre, picture Marie and Pierre Curie in lab coats at the Sorbonne, and imagine the stories etched in stone within the cemeteries of Père Lachaise and Montparnasse. . . . Dance with Leslie Caron in Vincente Minnelli's *An American in Paris*, scamper with Audrey Tautou in Jean-Pierre Jeunet's *Amélie*, but don't flirt with Jeanne Moreau in François Truffaut's *Jules and Jim*. . . . Saunter along the Seine, crossing two of thirty-seven bridges joining Paris's left and right banks: the oldest, Le Pont Neuf, and newest, Passerelle Simone de Beauvoir. . . . Continuing your stroll, watch the riverside vendor create your crêpe, bargain for a book from a *bouquiniste*, and light a candle in the Cathedral of Notre Dame on historic Île de la Cité. . . .

Simone de Beauvoir's funeral on April 19, 1986, confirms that her childhood dream of personal freedom came true. Flowers arrived from the large world she touched: publishers and diverse political groups, international women's health organizations, and American university students grateful for her writings. Some five thousand people from all walks of life walked together through Paris streets filled with de Beauvoir's presence as they made their pilgrimage to Montparnasse cemetery. She was at the forefront of French existentialism, a rebellious, flamboyant departure from analytical, depersonalized philosophy. All comers are welcome for breakfast or lunch to philosophize at the *café-philos* flourishing in France today, these lively gatherings reminiscent of the heady debates enjoyed by de Beauvoir and friends in their own *café philosophiques*. Tonight she waits for us at Les Deux Magots.

No

When life's sweet juice goes undrunk, "disillusioned indifference" (*Ethics*) can worm its way into any heart. Child philosophers explain that "you can die without being dead." Barely stopping them before they can give me quite pointed examples, I listen to varied descriptions of how "at some definite point people get gloomy." De Beauvoir agrees with these youthful observations. Holding forth at her regular table, she reveals our evening plan. To start, we must unravel the disastrous homespun lie we tell ourselves when we pretend that we are not free and the future holds no promise. Like a spider enclosed in a web of its own making, negative patterns of behavior strap us down. Unpleasant though it may be, by exposing very specific ways in which we keep "bad faith" (*Ethics*) with ourselves and others, we win back our lives. Here we go—diners trading admissions of pessimism and cow-

ardice, snapshots of freedom forsaken. Gulp. Not a pretty sight, not yet.

> ### THE IDEA OF ENTERING UPON A LIFE OF MY OWN INTOXICATED ME.
>
> SIMONE DE BEAUVOIR,
> *Memoirs of a Dutiful Daughter*

I stereotype. Slapping a label on your back without the nerve to look at you full on, I steal your personality. You "become a thing" (*The Second Sex*), set in stone by my self-serving branding—geek and jock, tomboy and sissy, fatty and bony, dark and light, wealthy and poor, skinhead and preppy, disabled and gifted, elderly and callow. . . . Your behavior and my reaction are predetermined. "Not capable of existing without a guarantee" (*Ethics*), I prefabricate a ready-made life tucked inside these chilly cubbyholes.

I fulfill other's expectations. Whether real or imagined, I long for anyone's approval. Took the job you wanted for me . . . broke up with the guy you disliked . . . dropped plans to leave home . . . finally lost my accent . . . entered politics like you . . . hid my partner from your parents. I walk the path downtrodden, wearing shoes that aren't mine, moving with "pure mechanical gestures" (*Ethics*).

I force my will. Hey, I give in to others so you'll kowtow to me. I coaxed my kid into marrying the pretty girl (he didn't tell me he loved someone else). I avoid dinner with my mom's new boyfriend (they hold hands). I'm put off by students sporting body piercings (I overlook their raised hands). I find a way not to rent to foreigners (you can always tell).

I am an actor. I star in the victim role. Sure, everybody has troubles, but not like mine. Things happen *to* me: The deadline passed before I turned in my application. I ran into the back of the car because the sun blinded me. He left me because he couldn't put up with my moods. The devil made me do it.

Though de Beauvoir loves our conversation, we don't like us at all. Too much! Taking the cuffs off our wrists, I'm jumping off this not merry-go-round. Foolish habits beg to be broken. I'll catch each stereotype and bring myself up short. Rather than imposing my will, I'll leave your life to you. How about that? I won't cave into someone else's prospects for me because inner strength will buttress my life. I'll quit that tiresome acting business and live my autobiography "in pride and joy" (*Ethics*). I'll dare myself to cry and care, laugh and try. Just the faintest rustlings of possibility heat my spirit. The thought of "maybe" thrills. Squandering nothing, I'll lavishly spend the time of my life, tipping generously.

The telling of one of my first-grade philosophy lessons rouses diners for more French philosophizing. While I was reading Shel Silverstein's *The Giving Tree* and showing the drawings on each page to the children, hysteria broke out at their first glimpse of a picture of hands clasped in front of the tree, the two bodies hidden behind the trunk. "Ha-ha! Bet that's the girl and that's the boy. No! You've got it backwards." We were stuck. "Don't turn the page yet," they commanded. Mercifully, Brian broke the spell: "It could be two girls or two boys, you know. Anything's possible."

No?

YES

Not for a moment does de Beauvoir overlook life's difficulty. Whether we endure ongoing hardship or suffer sudden catastrophe, she motions us forward with hearty assurance that we can win the match that is life. "It is because there are real dangers, real failures, and real earthly damnation that words like victory, wisdom, or joy have meaning" (*Ethics*). My dinner and classroom buddies prove her right. Meet some regular folk who "cast themselves into the world with a largeness of spirit" (*Ethics*). In existentialist philosophy as in life, actions speak louder than words. Add your stories to these. De Beauvoir cups an ear.

Four diners share the exhilaration of pushing past "my old self." A longtime social worker, never losing her collegiate passion for art, learns to fire up a kiln. Passing around her ceramic beauties, Peggy says "you never know" to a career change. Jake entertains the group with his trip for the ages, bringing his grandparents to meet their relatives on German soil. Though his friend/guide/translator canceled at the last moment, they pressed on, each moment another experiment, gleeful at successful nonverbal communication and discovery of centuries' deep ancestral roots. Butler's hiring as manager of a new restaurant stuns his friends. Interviewing five times, he insisted that his two previous failures in this position made him the ideal candidate, an expert at what not to do. Yes, some of our most positive steps forward have "begun by emphasizing the element of failure . . ." (*Ethics*). Like rungs on an extension ladder, our life experiences support us in the climb upward. Elizabeth holds high a photograph. Captivated as a high school senior by drawings of a double-ended sailing dory, she completed a boat-building class at age thirty-nine. The only female in the group, she was passed over as tools circulated and her input was ignored, but the seafaring urge trumped shyness. A few years later, her instructor guided her in dory construction. After wielding power saws and handsaws, block planes and drills, and sewing stitches with a sailmaker, Elizabeth, at forty-two, launched the *Pungoteague* on the Hudson River. Seconding de Beauvoir's stance that "the me-others relationship is indissoluble" (*Ethics*), another quarter's hold strokes foster freedom for others and at the same time liberate them. A beloved nurse practitioner musters the courage to leave her practice, choosing to be a constant presence in her children's young lives. An educator founds an alternative school, determined to find innovative approaches to reach lost adolescents. A college student works her way through school by tutoring children in a crime-riddled area, striving for a "communion of freedom" (*Ethics*), calling 911 as needed on brisk morning walks. A man looks back at his declaration of independence upon graduating from college, putting off his eventual corporate career for volunteer work in an impoverished Jamaican neighborhood. What did he learn as he built homes and kicked soccer balls? "Everything—that people deserve help, that power corrupts, that crime is understandable, that what matters is doing your best to make nightmares less scary." Yes, de Beauvoir clinks a glass, "only the freedom of others keeps each one of us from hardening" (*Ethics*).

Who hasn't felt the pang of despair at too-long odds? Despite and to spite difficulty, de Beauvoir maintains that we "must assume even these misfortunes" (*Ethics*). The following daring trio, Jean, Robin, and Mary, shakes trouble by the tail. None of them finds their toughness special, but what splendid displays of "patience, courage, and fidelity" (*Ethics*). Both terrified and desperate to be with her dying mom, Jean never wavered in love. She entered into every wrenching, sacred moment. Robin pursued grueling physical therapy to outmaneuver scoliosis and now runs strongbacked marathons. She moved to a town knowing no one, developed the requisite business savvy to open a fitness studio, and seized the right moment to expand her business during the recession.

In April a woman slid from her motorized scooter onto an exercise machine, pedaling with effort. Months passed and faithful gym goers could count on seeing her, smiling and stretching, arms rowing and legs pressing. Watching her progress was the best part of my workout. On a December day, glory painted Mary's face. Hold-ing on to the railing, using two crutches wherever the railing stopped, she walked a mile around the track to celebrate her seventy-first birthday, her doctor joining her for the last lap. Mary's largest hurdle now is being interrupted by people (like me) wanting a brushing of her stardust. Born with cerebral palsy and nurtured by a mother who "let me fall and watched me pick myself up, my biggest fan," she danced at her high school prom "in my own way" and walked unassisted across the stage to receive her diploma. Hankering for independence, she trained for a job as a computer programmer and, quick with her hands, rose to supervisor. Mary managed the long distance between offices with the scooter, a bargain that atrophied her muscles. "My goal is to walk on my own like fifty years ago. It's not too late to make the muscles live again."

We "dash off toward the future . . . which is the meaning of tomorrow" (*Ethics*).

Double dog daring you.

AND YOUR TOPIC FOR DINNER CONVERSATION IS

"Regardless of the staggering dimensions of the world about us, the density of our ignorance, the risks of catastrophes to come, and our individual weakness within the immense collectivity, the fact remains that we are absolutely free today if we choose . . ." (*Ethics*). There you have it! What do you recognize now about unnecessary naysaying? Be specific. Talk about what saying YES will bring to your life.

THE DOORBELL RINGS

Don't be deterred by one connoisseur's claim that "good Calvados is never sold legally" ("The Afterglow," *Secret Ingredients: The New Yorker Book of Food and Drink*), and

enjoy a small-production variety picked out by a volunteering guest. Distilled from cider rather than wine, this caramel-colored apple brandy from the Normandy region, at its best, smells like a musty cellar in a small French village. Guests can select from among a wide variety of buttery French cheeses while swooping up plenty of baguettes, both mainstays in French spreads. One diner (hopefully) brings a simple green salad to be accompanied by another's Dijon mustard vinaigrette. Bottles of Côtes du Rhône or other Rhône-style red wines make a fine match for this braised beef dish. (Hint!)

Strains of "gypsy jazz" (jazz *manouche*), pioneered by guitarist Django Reinhardt and violinist Stéphane Grappelli, lure you in from the "Black Night." Their "Swing Guitars" filled 1930s cabarets and kept heads bopping well into de Beauvoir's heyday, serving up treats of "Improvisation no. 5" such as "How High the Moon" and "C Jam Blues." A familiar voice puts the official stamp on your French evening. Who else but Édith Piaf, the "Little Sparrow," owns "Hymne à l'amour," "Milord," "La Vie en Rose," "Le Vieux Piano," and "L'accordéoniste"? Fresh-fingered jazz pianist Martial Solal asks, "Have You Met Miss Jones?" His "Bluesine" slows the tempo, encouraging you to begin your daring discussion right now rather than "Round About Midnight."

Pick your partner in Camille Saint-Saëns's *Le Carnaval des Animaux* (*Carnival of the Animals*). Tortoise, swan, lion, kangaroo, elephant, hen and rooster combo, lion, wild asses, or cuckoo, these fourteen short movements add a playful touch to your talk of adventure. When the parade ends, revolutionary composer and dynamic personality Erik Satie offers the pure pleasure of his *Trois Gymnopédies*. Absorb their tender rendering by countryman/pianist Jean-Yves Thibaudet, as well as any of Satie's *Gnossiennes*. Picking up the pace a bit, Claude Bolling teams with Yo-Yo Ma in Bolling's composition *Suite for Cello and Jazz Piano Trio*. Bol-

ling's piano continually reinvents itself and Ma's usually classical cello turns to jazz, their collaboration supporting the heart of your discussion. Dig deep with "Concertante," slip into "Baroque in Rhythm," and breeze to the finish line with a "Cello Fan" at your back. Now, blast "The Finale" of Saint-Saëns's *Carnival*.

Vocalist and civil rights activist Josephine Baker walked with Dr. King and served in the French Resistance in World War II. Refusing to perform for segregated audiences, she found a home in Paris and was eventually buried in her adopted country with full military honors. Listen to this icon of daring in her "La Conga Blicoti," "Dis-Moi Josephine?" and "Peg De Mon Coeur." No wonder she could sing "I'm Feelin' Like a Million." Jean-Luc Ponty's jazzed violin salutes your determination to venture into "New Country," taking the group for a stroll through "The Gardens of Babylon" and sending you "Wandering on the Milky Way." After (never with) dessert, relax with small cups of black coffee (*café noir*). French/Armenian humanitarian, the multitalented Charles Aznavour looms large on international entertainment and political stages. Let French sounds wash over you with songs from his *Toujours* . . . perhaps "Va," "Ce Printemps-Là," "Que J'aime J'aime Ça," "Les Jours," and the unforgettable "Elle" performed in duet with Thomas Dutronc.

SALMON COOKED ON A BED OF SALT

Cooked in a cast-iron skillet over a layer of salt, this simple, two-ingredient salmon appetizer crackles and pops as high heat generated by the salt sears the fish from the bottom up. What better way to taxi your supper club back to the smoky jazz haunts of de Beauvoir's day. Crack a window!

PREPARATION: 25 minutes

1½ pounds skin-on center-cut salmon fillet (cut to fit pan if needed)

Salt and pepper, to taste

2 cups coarse-grained salt, or enough to cover the bottom of your skillet to ½-inch depth

Crackers, for serving

1. Using paper towels, pat the salmon dry and season with salt and pepper.

2. Turn on an exhaust fan. In a cast-iron or heavy-bottomed large skillet with a lid, distribute the coarse-grained salt in an even ½-inch layer and heat over medium-high heat until just smoky, 3 to 5 minutes.

3. Place the salmon, skin side down, on the salt and cover the skillet with the lid. Cook, without turning, until medium-rare, approximately 8 minutes. Remove from the heat with the lid still on and let stand 1 to 2 minutes.

4. Carefully lift the salmon off of the skin and transfer it to a serving platter. Discard the skin. Slice the salmon and serve on crackers.

POT-AU-FEU

Literally "pot on the fire," this classic dish of simmering hearty ingredients epitomizes the French approach to rustic cooking. Often referred to as the "eternal pot" ("The Afterglow") because clever cooks continue to replenish the rich base with vegetables and meat for subsequent meals, a pot-au-feu is the French version of boiled beef. De Beauvoir considered the trusty pot-au-feu her specialty and served it to fellow existentialists Camus and Sartre, frequent dinner companions. You'll want to start preparing the pot-au-feu at least five hours (and preferably a day) before your dinner. Ask the butcher to tie up the roast portion of the beef so that it maintains its shape during cooking and final carving. A very large pot is needed for the sizable quantity of meat, liquid, and vegetables used in making the broth. If you do not have a pot this size, the meats, liquids, and vegetables can be divided among two or more smaller ones.

PREPARATION: 5–6 hours (1 hour active)

3 pounds tied beef roast (from rump)

3 pounds bone-in beef short ribs

7 quarts cold water (or a combination of 3 quarts chicken stock and 4 quarts water)

4 large leeks, white and light green parts only, halved lengthwise and washed thoroughly

8 large carrots, peeled

4 celery stalks, cut in half

4 medium onions, peeled

3 bay leaves

5 sprigs each of fresh parsley and thyme, or 1 teaspoon each dried

1 tablespoon kosher salt, or to taste

5–6 whole black peppercorns

2 pounds additional root vegetables (parsnips, turnips, rutabagas, leeks, potatoes, carrots, etc.), peeled and chopped into attractive quarters or eighths to create pieces approximately 2 inches long, or if appropriate (e.g., leeks), tied into bundles with kitchen twine to preserve a tidy appearance for serving

1 baguette, sliced into ½-inch-thick slices, rubbed with a peeled, whole garlic clove, and toasted

Selection of condiments, such as cornichons (small pickles), coarse sea salt, whole-grain mustard, and horseradish

1. Place the beef roast and short ribs in a large stockpot. Add water until the meat is just covered and bring to a boil. Skim the accumulated fat off the top. Drain the meat in a colander and rinse with cold water. Rinse out the pot. If you are short on time, you may omit this step, but your broth will not be as clear.

2. Return the meat to the pot, add the 7 quarts of cold water (or water and stock), and bring to a boil. Once boiling, immediately reduce the heat to medium-low and skim the accumulated fat.

3. Add the leeks, carrots, celery, onions, bay leaves, parsley, and thyme to the pot and return to a boil. Immediately lower the heat to a simmer. Skim the surface again and then season with the salt and peppercorns. Cover with the lid very slightly ajar so that steam can escape, and cook at a low simmer for 3 to 4 hours, depending on the cut of your meat, until the roast is tender. If you are preparing ahead, cool and refrigerate overnight. Otherwise proceed to step 5.

4. The next day, remove the accumulated fat from the surface of the chilled broth. Gently reheat the broth, but do not boil. Using a slotted spoon, remove the vege-

tables from the broth and discard. Remove the meat and strain all of the broth. Proceed to step 6.

5. If you did not prepare the broth the night before, remove the vegetables from the broth using a slotted spoon and discard. Remove the meat and strain all of the broth.

6. Place the meat and one to two cups of broth from the pot in a covered baking dish to keep warm while the root vegetables cook. Add the root vegetables to the remaining broth and simmer to the desired tenderness, 20 to 30 minutes.

7. Remove the bones from the short ribs, slice the roast, and arrange the meats on a platter. Remove the root vegetables from the broth with a slotted spoon and add them to the platter with the meats. Drizzle a small amount of the broth over the meats and vegetables. Now! Guests may fill their bowls with meat and vegetables, ladling hot broth as they go. Baguette slices and condiments complete your feast.

CLEMENTINE SOUFFLÉ

Soufflé-making follows a simple formula of a flavor base and whipped egg whites. The clementine, available from late October through early February, is the tiniest of the mandarin oranges, small, usually seedless, and very sweet. Most experts agree that it's best to work quickly (yet gently) during preparation, then sit back and wait for the sugary eruption. To ward off any uncertainty, watch the master of fearlessness, Julia Child, in action in her 1972 Cheese Soufflé video. To minimize the cook's time away from the guests, some preparation before their arrival will not harm the soufflé. Steps 2 through 4 can be done earlier that day. If you refrigerate the mixture, take it out when the doorbell rings.

PREPARATION: 1 hour, 30 minutes (15 minutes active)

1 tablespoon melted butter

⅔ cup plus 2 tablespoons sugar

1¼ cups clementine juice

1 tablespoon cornstarch

2 teaspoons grated clementine zest

4 large egg yolks

6 large egg whites

½ teaspoon cream of tartar

1. Preheat the oven to 375 degrees.

2. Prepare a 2- to 2½-quart (7½ to 8 inches in diameter) soufflé dish. If you don't have one, any high-sided ceramic or glass dish can be substituted. Brush the bottom and sides, including the rim, with the melted butter and coat the sides with the 2 tablespoons sugar, knocking out any excess. Refrigerate the dish until needed.

3. In a small bowl, whisk together 2 tablespoons of the clementine juice with the cornstarch and set aside. In a small saucepan over medium-high heat, bring 1 cup clementine juice, 1/3 cup of the sugar, and the zest to a boil and stir until the sugar is dissolved. Add the cornstarch mixture and whisk briefly, until thickened. Remove from the heat and whisk in the remaining 2 tablespoons clementine juice. Cool to lukewarm before proceeding to the next step.

4. In a large bowl, with an electric mixer at medium speed, beat the egg yolks and clementine mixture until it lightens in color. Wash and dry the beaters.

5. Using the electric mixer with clean beaters, beat the egg whites with the cream of tartar on medium speed until soft peaks form. Gradually beat in the remaining 1/3 cup sugar and continue beating until stiff peaks form and the whites are glossy.

6. With a rubber spatula, carefully fold in 1/2 cup of the beaten egg whites into the egg yolk mixture. Repeat with the remaining egg whites, taking care not to overmix. Scoop the mixture into the prepared dish.

7. Place the soufflé in the middle of the oven and bake for 40 to 45 minutes, until the soufflé is beginning to set around the edges.

8. Serve immediately.

FRANCE TO GO

Read Victor Hugo's *Les Misérables* and his short, striking poem "Demain, dès l'aube" ("Tomorrow, at Dawn"), scribble notes in the margin of *The Diary of Anaïs Nin, Vol One, 1931–1934*, and reward yourself with a lime blossom–soaked madeleine while reading Marcel Proust's *Swann's Way* from *Remembrance of Things Past*. . . . Listen to Serge Gainsbourg's "Je l'Aime Moi Non Plus," Mylène Farmer's "Désenchantée," and Georges Bizet's *Carmen*. . . . Hear the sounds of sliding feet and thudding bounces on the red clay courts of Roland Garros while remembering tennis great Suzanne Lenglen's play at the French Open. . . . Travel to Mont Blanc, Bretagne beaches, Avignon ruins, Bordeaux and Champagne vineyards, the châteaux of Chambord and Chenonceau in the Loire Valley, and back in time to Christmas Eve, 1914, in director Christian Carion's *Joyeux Noël*. . . . Absorb classic French cinema in Jean Renoir's *La Grande Illusion* and Louis Malle's *Au Revoir les Enfants (Good-bye, Children)*, visit Provence in Claude Berri's *Jean de Florette/Manon des Sources* and Saint-Tropez in Edouard Molinaro's *La Cage aux Folles*. . . .

RESOURCES

PHILOSOPHY

The Ethics of Ambiguity by Simone de Beauvoir, translated by Bernard Frechtman.

Memoirs of a Dutiful Daughter by Simone de Beauvoir, translated by James Kirkup.

The Second Sex by Simone de Beauvoir, translated by H. M. Parshley.

MUSIC

Le Quintet du Hot Club de France by Django Reinhardt and Stéphane Grappelli: "Black Night," "Swing Guitars," "Improvisation no. 5," "How High the Moon," "C Jam Blues."

30th Anniversaire by Édith Piaf: "Hymne à l'amour," "Milord," "La Vie en Rose," "Le Vieux Piano," "L'accordéoniste."

Bluesine by Martial Solal: "Have You Met Miss Jones?" "Bluesine," "Round About Midnight."

Le Carnaval des Animaux by Camille Saint-Saëns, London Sinfonietta, Charles Dutoit, conducting.

The Magic of Satie by Erik Satie, Jean-Yves Thibaudet, piano: *Trois Gymnopédies, Gnossiennes.*

Suite for Cello and Jazz Piano Trio by Claude Bolling, Claude Bolling, piano; Yo-Yo Ma, cello: "Concertante," "Baroque in Rhythm," "Cello Fan."

Centenary Tribute: Songs from 1930–1953 by Josephine Baker: "La Conga Blicoti," "Dis-Moi Josephine?" "Peg De Mon Coeur," "I'm Feelin' Like a Million."

Imaginary Voyage by Jean-Luc Ponty: "New Country," "The Gardens of Babylon," "Wandering on the Milky Way."

Toujours by Charles Aznavour: "Va," "Ce Printemps-Là," "Que J'aime J'aime Ça," "Les Jours," "Elle" with Thomas Dutronc.

FOOD

Secret Ingredients: The New Yorker Book of Food and Drink, edited by David Remnick: "The Afterglow" by A. J. Liebling.

La Bonne Cuisine de Madame E. Saint-Ange: The Original Companion for French Home Cooking by Madame E. Saint-Ange.

`The French Chef:` "Cheese Soufflé," with Julia Child, 1972.

Thanksgiving

A festive atmosphere greeted this book in the-making at every turn. What a jolly go round and round I had with the many enthusiastic people who pulled up chairs to this philosopher's worktable. A burst of gratitude sent to each and every one. Now, drum roll, please:

A GLASS RAISED HIGH OVERHEAD TO:

Kitchen Gurus: pioneering Head Chef Paige Turner, her painstaking research matching her culinary artistry, and my legion of high-spirited sous-chefs, their flour-covered fingers adjusting temperatures while sampling each dish, offering invaluable suggestions and home (mine) delivery. And a loud ring of the dinner gong for Letty Macdonald and Charlotte Self, good cooks and better friends.

Players in the Band: finger-snapping lead Kristen Brooking backed by a trio of big boppers, Brian Keena, Jonathan Mudd, and Kay Bethea.

Carnival Barkers: chief bellower Jan Kilfeather-Mackey joined by cosuppliers of support and essential intangibles Piotr Altana, Amy Gillespie, Matthew Mudd, Beryl Solla, Grace Carpenter, Jean Burke, Isaiah

Reynolds, Irina Timchenko, Susan Johnson, Julie Colaw, Mac Macdonald, Kris Swanson, Floyd Miller, Kit Decker, Will Moncure, Susan Moss, and my agent, lo, now three books, Patty Moosbrugger.

A STANDING-UP-IN-MY-CHAIR-ON-TIPTOES TOAST TO:

Andrew Yackira: my editor at Tarcher/Penguin, and vigilant shepherd of our book's journey to publication—talented, affable, and hilarious—an author's lucky day dressed in seersucker.

Jacob Neal: my Man Friday (and Saturday through Thursday).

Andy Kaufman: fellow writer, my monthly partner in putting feet up and stoking creative fires.

Julie Gronlund: my sharp-penciled lookout, escorting the book as it danced its way home.

Jay and Betsy Dalgliesh: best friends whose presence completes every dinner gathering.

E. J. Mudd: my aunt, who taught me the timeless joy of memorizing poetry and how to eat an artichoke.

Maria Ruth: my cousin, but more like a solicitous and encouraging sibling as we grow into the steel-bonded sisterhood, as best we can, shared by our mothers.

June and Mac: my parents. Mac, with Irish eyes smiling, the master of the backyard grill, much-loved and loving philosopher-in-residence. And, June, whose kitchen welcomes everyone home with the jingle of backdoor bells and whose style captures every chapter in this book.

About the Author

MARIETTA MCCARTY is the author of *Little Big Minds: Sharing Philosophy with Kids* (a *New York Times* Extended List best seller) and *How Philosophy Can Save Your Life: 10 Ideas That Matter Most* (Winner of the Nautilus Book Award). For more than two decades she taught philosophy at Piedmont Virginia Community College in Charlottesville, Virginia. Now a writer by trade, she travels around the country, speaking with groups of all ages and hosting lively events that celebrate the art of clear thinking. Visit Marietta online at:

www.mariettamccarty.com

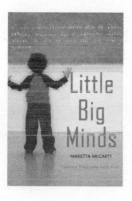

If you enjoyed this book, visit

www.tarcherbooks.com

and sign up for Tarcher's e-newsletter to receive
special offers, giveaway promotions, and
information on hot upcoming releases.

TARCHER
PENGUIN

Great Lives Begin with Great Ideas

Connect with the Tarcher Community

• • •

Stay in touch with favorite authors!
Enter weekly contests!
Read exclusive excerpts!
Voice your opinions!

Follow us

 Tarcher Books

 @TarcherBooks

If you would like to place a bulk order
of this book, call 1-800-847-5515.